Haiku Guy

a novel by

David G Lanoue

Soffietto Editions

Haiku Guy

ISBN 1-893959-13-9
© 2000 David G. Lanoue
A Soffietto Edition

Red Moon Press
P.O. Box 2461
Winchester VA
22604-1661 USA
redmoon@shentel.net

for "Chaz," "Paul,"
"Melanie," and "Micky" . . .
you know who you are!

Haiku Guy

PART ONE

Once Upon a Time

IN OLD JAPAN, deep in mountains by a lake that froze half the year, where loads of snow piled like top hats on the heads of weary cows; where gray slush filled deep ditches along the Shogun's snaking highway to more important places; in a land of snow where snow melted to the whispery tune of mid-summer's enormous mosquitoes; in a poor province, a downtrodden land where farmers tried to forget the rice tax as they passed the *sake*, sang the songs, and took turns simmering in hot tubs, cauldrons of steamy water that turned grimmer and browner with each bony, naked bather. It was here, in a village that has never shown up on a Western map and probably never will, in a small, thatched farmhouse on a hill of snow-dusted pines. Heaven's river of stars, the Milky Way, sluiced through the blackness above, pouring cold light onto an old, cracked, soot-blackened door.

A man stooped over his walking stick, shiny-bald, pot-bellied, boots skidding on ice. After forty years of wandering the countryside, crisscrossing the provinces, an aimless drifter, a wind-blown spirit, was home.

He called himself Cup-of-Tea; this was his pen name. Or you might say it was his bamboo-brush name, since he didn't own a pen. In any case, it was the name he scribbled in blotchy calligraphy on the rice paper of fat diaries, crammed with thousands of one-line, one-breath, epics . . . for Cup-of-Tea was a poet of haiku.

You might be wondering: What is haiku? Now there's a blank not easily filled. To do so, we must observe Cup-of-Tea closely: how he slurps his pond-snail soup, how he pisses zigzag out the back door writing riddles in dawn ice, how he nibbles his noodles by the light of a solitary lamp in deepest winter seclusion.

We'll watch. We'll listen. Maybe, we'll learn.

Buck Teeth

"Excuse me, sir, but is it true you are a poet?"

Cup-of-Tea gazed down from his perch high in the black pine. Someone peered up at him through wet branches, more boy than man. More-Boy-Than-Man was dressed in the typical dull clothes of the province and conspicuously polite. Unsure whether to bow or to gaze up at the grown man swaying in the branches above him, More-Boy-Than-Man alternated between deferential bows to the earth and inquisitive glimpses to the sky, where Cup-of-Tea lazily sprawled.

"Yes, boy. I'm Cup-of-Tea."

"Nice, nice to meet you!" He bowed once more toward the puddled mud, and then, craning his neck way back, broke into a huge smile of misplaced teeth.

"I'm Deba, village poet!" he gushed. "Nice to meet

you, Master Cup-of-Tea!"

"Village poet, eh? And with a fine bamboo-brush name. Did you give yourself this name?"

Deba in Japanese means "Sticking-Out-Teeth." The closest translation in English would be "Buck-Teeth."

Buck-Teeth was politely inspecting his muddy clogs, so Cup-of-Tea could not hear his reply. It didn't matter. Cup-of-Tea could guess the story. This bright peasant lad, son of a farmer whose universe stretched as far as the property line, had been teased all his life because he was gentle, because he had sticking-out teeth, and because, thanks to inexplicable karma from the misty beginnings of time all the way up to the present moment in which he now stood, not quite a man, under a rain-slicked black pine in front of Cup-of-Tea's house . . . Buck-Teeth was a poet, or at least, believed he was.

The older poet clambered down to terra firma and invited the younger one into the house. Cup-of-Tea, true to his name, served tea. They knelt across from each other and sipped.

"So, what kind of poet are you, Buck-Teeth?"

"A poet of haiku, sir. But . . ." He stared into his tea, as if ashamed. "My family needs me in the fields. Or else I'd do what *you* did, leave this shitty town and go to Edo!"

Cup-of-Tea slurped his green brew, his mind flitting over well-worn images of his arrival in Edo four decades ago. He had quickly joined a horde of ragtag street children from the sticks. They had begged and thieved to stay alive. Most were unwanted back home; all were soon disillusioned. The Shogun's capital turned out not to be the city of gold they had dreamed of, but a sprawling, disease-ridden, foul-smelling, rat-in-fested sewer of taverns and brothels, where mad-drunk samurai made geisha scream and exercised their legal right to cut, even kill, any peasant boy they didn't like the looks of.

"Ah, yes...Edo." Cup-of-Tea broke the long silence of his reverie. "But you don't need to go there to write haiku."

"Yes. But Master Cup-of-Tea, *you* did!"

Cup-of-Tea changed the subject. "Recite me a poem, your best poem."

Buck-Teeth's face brightened with wide, sparkling eyes, teeth thrusting out in a smile. He wore his heart on his sleeve, as they say, the emotion of each moment easily readable in his open-book face.

"With pleasure, sir! I wrote this haiku one full-moon night in my father's rice field. A cat was staring at me from a ditch. At first I didn't know it was dead. Its eyes reflected the moonlight. Then I saw its body was stiff, half of it under the black water. Well, here it is:

> "in the dead cat's eyes
> harvest
> moons."

Cup-of-Tea closed his eyes as tightly as he could, fighting an inward battle. He fought this battle so in-tensely, his face turned plum-blossom crimson while

Buck-Teeth gasped in terror. Had his poem been so bad as to send the sensitive master into a seizure? Cup-of-Tea's face clenched in such a tense, red grimace, it reminded Buck-Teeth of those scowling guardian monsters who flank the gates of temples.

Finally, composed but still flushed, the master opened his eyes. He refilled their cups with hot green tea, but said nothing. Buck-Teeth's haiku dangled in the air like a desperate question.

Then Cup-of-Tea broke the silence with a simple sentence that made the young poet's easy-to-read face dazzle once again, all shining eyes and pushed-out, smiling overbite.

"Buck-Teeth, you will be my student."

Stop Look Listen

I LEARNED the cardinal rules of street crossing in elementary school. From second grade on, I attended a Catholic school in my hometown of Omaha, Nebraska. In those days, nuns still wore black, medieval robes with flowing veils. Every day or two, they herded us double-file across the street to the church for mass or confession—or just for the hell of it, because they practiced, and demanded, daily, conspicuous piety. We'd stop at the curb, and every time before crossing over to the church or back to the school, we'd hear a life-saving litany recited at the top of Sister Agoniste's drill sergeant lungs: "Stop, look, and listen, children!"

This, it turned out, was my first lesson in the art of haiku.

***

Buck-Teeth didn't quite grasp this lesson, as he squatted in the weeds by the grain shed, watching that snail. He expected that, any minute, Cup-of-Tea would look up and transform the creeping critter into a brilliant poem, and they would move on, or at least eat breakfast. But nothing of the sort happened. They just watched and watched and watched and watched.

Buck-Teeth was bored and confused. And the evil little snail, as if for spite, kept taking breaks to catch its breath, or poke all its four antenna-eyes up to check the breeze, or maybe it was narcoleptic, nodding off for quick naps as it slimed along. When it finally, slowly shimmied into a crevice under the grain shed, Buck-Teeth let out a cheer.

Cup-of-Tea said nothing. No brilliant poem, no verbal lesson expounded on the art of haiku. Their long morning's exercise of snail watching remained, to Buck-Teeth, an enigma.

Stop, look, listen.

All that week Cup-of-Tea and Buck-Teeth had witnessed all sorts of slow things. Before the snail on the plank ordeal, they had whiled away a whole afternoon listening to grass grow. Finally, at dusk, Buck-Teeth thought he heard the pushing-up blades, a faint squeak. The day before that, at dawn, they had waded into a soaking field of grass and butterbur, where they sat to watch the dewdrops, some of them huge enough to fill teacups, slowly, slowly, *slowly* evaporate. Cup-of-Tea was delighted; Buck-Teeth developed a rash on his butt. Day before *that*, when they happened upon a frog in the grove behind the radish field on the hill, Cup-of-Tea had crouched low for a staring contest. The eye battle had lasted forever, it seemed to Buck-Teeth. Neither frog nor poet blinked. It was an honorable draw.

Buck-Teeth didn't yet understand the necessity of stopping, looking, and listening. The good nuns of St. Bernard's could have drilled this into him by age ten, had he but been born in another place, another time. However, being the son of piss-poor farmers in a piss-poor province deep in the snowy mountains of Old Japan, nothing in his background had prepared the boy to make sense of his master's odd exercises.

When Buck-Teeth came home each night, his father would ask how the lessons were coming. His father accepted the fact that Buck-Teeth was learning the art of haiku from Cup-of-Tea, and he grudgingly approved—so long as all the chores got done. Every night, before venturing into the dark fields to make up for time spent at Cup-of-Tea's poetry school, Buck-Teeth invented all kinds of fantastic stories to tell his father. He was frankly embarrassed to admit that he had spent the morning watching a snail or the afternoon staring down a frog.

"Today Master Cup-of-Tea taught me how to interpret the language of the cuckoo," he would say. Or "This morning Master Cup-of-Tea showed me how to write poems so airy-light we had to weigh them down with pebbles to keep the ink from floating off!"

As it turned out, Buck-Teeth's wonderful stories were wasted on his father, who would have humphed and snorted just as skeptically had he been told the truth of how his son had wasted another working day.

Lord Kaga

LORD KAGA was in love.

Earlier that morning, he had climbed, alone, to the topmost level of Matsumoto Castle, his bare feet padding quickly and stealthily up the worn, wood steps. Now he knelt by one of the tall, narrow windows from which archers had once aimed arrows at armies in the dewy field below, skewering men and horses with cruel accuracy. But Lord Kaga was not thinking of heroic wars this morning. He watched the sun rise over rumpled, blue mountains to the east, a mother deer with her fawn splashing in purple shadows. The sigh he sighed was a love sigh.

He spread rice paper on the floor, mixed a puddle of fragrant black ink with a fresh tear, and dipped the horsehair tip of his thick bamboo brush in the poignant mixture. He started writing.

***

From their perch high on the hill behind "Trash House," as Cup-of-Tea liked to call his abode, master and student watched the arrival of Lord Kaga and his magnificent entourage in the village below. For Buck-Teeth, the event was turning out to be yet another of his master's dreary lessons in stop, look, listen. For two solid hours, Lord Kaga's long, long retinue filed into town—samurai on horseback and an army of servants toting chests, furniture, birdcages, baskets, potted trees, and fancy palanquins in which rode Lord Kaga's geisha. On and on they came, a grand entry into such a small town, its straw-packed street lined with motionless, groveling villagers. They dared not look up at the terrible *daimyo* who sat on the village headman's verandah, lording over the arrival of his moveable household.

Just as Buck-Teeth's patience reached an end, the last of the attendants rounded the bend of misty hills. Cup-of-Tea sighed, and said,

"They even haul the mist!
Lord Kaga's
men."

Children sang their special song of welcome with shrill voices, while Lord Kaga stared into space. The headman, trembling, kowtowed at the *daimyo's* feet. When the children stopped singing, everyone in the village, which in one afternoon had quadrupled in population, breathlessly awaited Lord Kaga's words.

The fearsome provincial lord at last deigned to address the headman who cowered like a cockroach begging to be crushed. But his words shocked and mystified the headman and every villager within earshot.

"Take me to the poet, Cup-of-Tea!"

Write

NOW YOU ARE READY to write your first haiku.

Unfortunately, no one can tell you what to write about, nor when, *precisely*, to begin, because this could result in a disastrous forcing of the moment. You'll just have to stop, look, listen, and—when you feel it's time—write.

Take, for example, Cup-of-Tea's haiku about Lord Kaga's grand entrance into the village, the long, long train of attendants hauling junk and birds and humanity—and even, it seemed, the mist that dragged behind them into town:

> they even haul the mist!
> Lord Kaga's
> men

Buck-Teeth was amazed at how spontaneously the master had exhaled the poem into the air, into being, after their week of silence: watching snails, staring at frogs, observing gallons of dewdrops burn to nothingness. It had taken a whole lot of silence for the right words to arise.

This phenomenon of long silence shattered by a burst of unexpected words is quite familiar to me. Before I began this text, I had kept silent for years and years, as far as book-writing goes. My last opus, *Garn the Cave Man*, I composed in grade school. In it, I chronicled the adventures of Garn, cave man *extraordinaire*. Each chapter of that novel detailed a thrilling episode in Garn's prehistoric struggle for survival: "Garn Battles the Tyrannosaurus," "Garn Fights the Giant Tarantula," and so on. Halfway through the book, Garn discovered the love of his life: his future cave wife, Lula. He saved her from all sorts of cranky dinosaurs, and they set up house in the cool darkness of a vast, stalactite-dripping cave. My own incipient puberty with all those warm, stirring hormones rushing through my bloodstream had an effect on the content of *Garn*. My hero's daily rescuing of Lula from hulking pythons and screeching pterodactyls invariably ended with the reunited couple's titillating embrace. And into the cave they'd vanish.

Adolescence brought an end to my career as a novelist. In those painful, tortured years, like Lord Kaga sobbing in the topmost archer's perch of Matsumoto Castle, I devoted myself exclusively to tear-drenched love poems.

But now, words are spilling onto the page almost too fast for my scratchy, blue Bic to capture them. These lessons are writing themselves, it seems, as if I'm just an entranced stenographer recording the

13

rapid-fire dictation of some invisible Buddha from beyond the physical plane.

How effortless, light, and buoyant my writing has become! As in Buck-Teeth's fantasy, I'm terrified that all the ink on this growing mound of paper on the table-top might rise into the air and float around my kitchen like crazy, blue spaghetti, until a strong breeze sucks the whole, swirling mess out the open window . . . blue gibberish vanishing in blue sky.

It could happen.

Lord Kaga (Again)

THE VILLAGE HEADMAN led Lord Kaga up the muddy, steep lane. The headman kept thinking that he was home in his futon, that he hadn't awakened yet this day, and this bizarre scene of which he found himself a part was occurring inside a dream. But, in case it wasn't a dream, he controlled himself and did not attempt his usual test that he used inside dreams to determine if indeed he was dreaming: that is, breast stroking into the sky.

It turned out, this was a prudent decision, for Lord Kaga had, indeed, arrived unexpectedly in the village that very afternoon, and his first and only command, though strange, indeed had been "Take me to the poet, Cup-of-Tea!"

Stifling his urge to swim into the clouds, the head-man banged on the soot-blackened door on the left-hand side of the farmhouse. The other front door—a neat, newly painted one to the right—flung open. The sour, wrinkled face of old Satsu, Cup-of-Tea's ancient stepmother, thrust out, then paled at the sight of mighty Kaga.

When Cup-of-Tea had returned to claim his ancestral home, at first there had been quite a flap. Stepmother Satsu would not budge from her insistence that her own, natural son, Senroku, deserved to inherit the place, since Cup-of-Tea had "abandoned" it. Senroku had never left; had remained there all his life, faithfully farming the family's buckwheat and rice fields in the misty pines. Finally, the village headman had come up with the brilliant idea of dividing the house in two, nailing a partition wall straight down the middle.

"Where's Cup-of-Tea?" the headman now demanded.

"Out back!" Satsu punctuated her reply by slamming the door so hard, the wind chimes that dangled above jumped their hook, crashing to the porch, tinking and tonking.

"Stay!" Lord Kaga commanded, leaving the headman and his samurai bodyguards standing in the front yard. He walked around to the back of the house alone.

Cup-of-Tea and Buck-Teeth were patting mudpies when Lord Kaga rounded the corner in a flowing rustle of emerald and blue silk. Buck-Teeth's easy-to-read face shifted, his bored expression replaced by one of stark terror. Cup-of-Tea, though, calmly continued slapping his fat, wet pie from one hand to the other, not bothering to look up.

15

"Mud dumplings, eh?" Lord Kaga crouched near the poet, leaning his face so close, his mint breath perfumed Cup-of-Tea's mucky confection. "We have missed you in the capital, Cup-of-Tea. I bring greetings from many friends. And one request. Come back to us! Why waste your time in this rat hole of a village when all Edo wants you back? They, I, have missed you, Cup-of-Tea!"

Buck-Teeth was groveling so low by now, his forearms sank into the squishy mud from which, moments before, he and Cup-of-Tea had been scooping material for pies—yet another baffling haiku lesson for which the younger poet had already invented a cover story to tell his dad: "Today Master Cup-of-Tea showed me how to read poems in the lights that dance and dart on the surface of tea!"

Cup-of-Tea, meanwhile, remained sitting and slapping his mud dumpling.

"This is my home," he said, finally.

"Well, it's your choice." Lord Kaga seemed eager to change the subject. "That's not the main reason I wanted to see you, old friend. I've just this morning written a haiku, and I beg you—tell me the truth—is it any good?"

The great lord of Shinano Province pulled out of his billowing, emerald-and-blue sleeve a roll of delicate, thin rice paper. He held this out to Cup-of-Tea, who made a motion to receive it with his right hand while offering his own mud pie with his left.

Seeing no way around it, Lord Kaga accepted the poet's pie with his free hand.

Cup-of-Tea took the poem, unrolled the crinkly paper it was scribbled on, and read Lord Kaga's haiku out loud:

broken again in spring
heart
in the rain

A long, long silence ensued. Buck-Teeth, pushing his chin deeper in the cold muck, tried not to breathe. Kaga's hand nervously squeezed the mud-dumpling, brown slivers of it oozing between his fingers.

Cup-of-Tea stood, abruptly, and walked to the nearby meadow where his half brother's cow was grazing. He selected a fresh cow pile, dropped Lord Kaga's rice-paper poem onto it, and tamped it in firmly with the heel of his clog.

Lord Kaga looked on, aghast. His fist closed tightly; the remnants of Cup-of-Tea's mud-pie splatted to the ground. Buck-Teeth, who had witnessed everything and would later write about it in his diary, held his breath.

Cup-of-Tea strolled back to his former spot and sat. Kaga stared coldly.

"You'll have to try harder," Cup-of-Tea said.

Then Lord Kaga and Cup-of-Tea, in the same seismic instant, erupted in wild laughter.

"Thank you, Master Cup-of-Tea!" Lord Kaga bellowed.

The Old Fart

To EVERYONE'S AMAZEMENT, Lord Kaga stayed in Kashiwabara village for weeks that stretched into months. Each morning he climbed the hill to visit Cup-of-Tea, a new tear-written love poem tucked inside his sleeve for the master's criticism.

The cow was kept busy. The yard behind Trash House filled with crumpled rice-paper poems stuck decoratively in shit piles. Senroku, Cup-of-Tea's half brother, didn't dare clean up the fluttering mess, afraid to touch the terrible daimyo's handiwork.

Buck-Teeth attended each of these morning sessions, with his father's enthusiastic approval. Buck-Teeth's father was thrilled to see his son hobnobbing with the High and Mighty One. Would not such fraternization lead to a court appointment? When Buck-Teeth came home at night, he discovered that his chores had already been done—by Dad, who insisted that he get to bed early for a good night's sleep. "Poetry," Buck-Teeth's father said gravely, "requires a rested mind."

It was Sixth Month, late summer by the old lunar calendar, when Lord Kaga presented to Cup-of-Tea his hundredth haiku in as many days.

Senroku's cow mooed in anticipation.

The haiku was the hundredth verse scribbled on the hundredth morning after his arrival in Kashiwabara. Lord Kaga hoped against hope that the auspicious number would bring him luck.

Earlier that day, as dawn's first bluish light had slanted through the window of his suite at the inn, Lord

Kaga had crept to his writing table, stepping gingerly over three nude concubines, asleep in the shadows—one, sucking her thumb like a child. Then, mixing ink with a few fresh tears, so easy to shed whenever he pictured in his mind his cruel mistress, Lady Plum, languishing so far away in the Shogun's capital; who after a hundred days still had not answered a single one of his passionate letters . . . he dipped the horse-hair tip of his bamboo brush into the black puddle and prayed for a miracle. None came. But ink was dripping, and so not to waste it, he dribbled out what was in his heart, not quite knowing what he was going to say till he watched it materialize on the page:

the old fart
stacks the winter
kindling

Now, behind Trash House, Cup-of-Tea unrolled Lord Kaga's rice-paper poem, as he always did, and read it out loud in one slowly exhaled breath, as he always did, pausing ever-so briefly after the first two phrases—like always. But this time something was different, indeed.

Buck-Teeth and Kaga knelt in expectant silence. Even Senroku's cow stood hushed, as if stunned by the daimyo's hundredth haiku.

"Yes," Cup-of-Tea said.

The Writing Group

I LIVE IN NEW ORLEANS, an old literary city draped with sad Spanish moss, where many are the writers and would-be writers. In my city, we would-be writers band together, much like the terrified, harassed urchins young Cup-of-Tea joined up with when he first stumbled, alone and penniless, through the great, yawning gates of Edo.

Writing groups meet once a week or twice a month, often in coffeehouses where hot java is pumped into veins, caffeine providing just the right manic buzz for us would-be writers to forget our natural shyness and, as we say, "share."

You, too, should form a writing group as soon as possible. Haiku is a social activity, like sex or bridge or singing karaoke songs at Happy Hour in a Bourbon Street pub.

My own writing group is eclectic. Melanie writes "true fictions" about her true-life experiences, like the summer she worked on a fishing boat in Alaska, or the year she taught sex education to villagers in Ghana. Melanie's real life, it turns out, is far more interesting than anything she could ever make up, so she just tells it like it was, and is.

Chaz is a science fiction/horror guy. He's composing a destined-to-be-movie novel about mutated monsters in his home state of Arkansas. In addition to lots of action and gore, his work-in-progress has its kinky side. When they have sex, six male monsters form a "pod" around each happy female. Melanie and Micky approve.

Speaking of Micky, she's working on a "novel" that's actually a jazzed-up or toned-down—we're not sure which—autobiography, a rambling, intellectual romance about a Jewish coed hitchhiking through Europe in the sixties. Her alter ego, also named Micky, happily gallivants about with all the swarthy, olive-skinned men with thick accents that she can handle—in exotic places like Trvesk and Bled and Istanbul. Like Chaz's monster women, Micky's Micky is getting plenty, to say the least. The group by now is so addicted to her story—after months of feeding on it, chapter by chapter—that every time she suffers her fit of writer's *angst* and threatens to burn it to ashes, we beg our Micky to keep her Micky going.

When I showed the group the first few chapters of this text, they were pleasantly surprised and eager to give feedback.

Melanie liked it, though she complained, as a woman, she didn't feel included, with all those "haiku guys" running around Old Japan. Did I plan to write in some three-dimensional female characters who didn't need men to define themselves?

"Why not?" I said, jotting down her suggestion.

Chaz spoke next. He asked why Cup-of-Tea's face had turned so bright red in Chapter 2, when he had grimaced like a gargoyle.

"Was Buck-Teeth's haiku that bad? Or was it so good that Cup-of-Tea was envious? Or was he angry?"

"I don't know," I admitted.

"Was it gas pain, perhaps?" Micky offered.

I shrugged. I really didn't know. Hadn't I made it clear to the group that all these tumbling-out words were emanating not from me, but from the Buddha?

Now it was Micky's turn to give feedback. She looked dead-on at me, her sparkling gray, been-everywhere eyes deconstructing me with their piercing gaze.

"There's no totalization in the text," she said.

"What?"

"This isn't a how-to book . . . or a novel. There's no totalization!"

I blinked, baffled.

While my writing group colleagues were as helpful as they could be last Thursday, I left the meeting with a queasy feeling in my stomach, as if a big, cold lump of jalapeño peppers were sloshing around inside it as I pedaled my bike down the darkening street. By the time I rolled under the Carrollton Avenue overpass, swerving 'round broken bottles and a sleeping wino, I realized what was wrong. Melanie, Micky, and Chaz weren't going to be much help until they saw for themselves, first-hand, where Cup-of-Tea was coming from. Then and there, I resolved to sneak my writing group into Old Japan at the earliest possible moment, perhaps in the next chapter.

Then, maybe, they'll understand.

Fireworks

THAT NIGHT, in celebration of his first approved poem, Lord Kaga hosted a fireworks display at the lake. The entire village was there, and all of Lord Kaga's army of attendants, "ooohing!" and "ahhhing!" as rockets burst in the sky, sapphire and blue sparks drifting lazily down to meet their reflections in the cold, black water.

Melanie, Chaz, and Micky were there, in period costume. Chaz was disguised as a wandering samurai, a long sword swinging jauntily from a scabbard that dangled from a shoulder. In one hand, he clutched a straw-wrapped jug of *sake*, from which he swigged after each explosion of *hana-bi* ("fire-blossoms") in the mountain sky. He was drunk and enjoying himself immensely in Old Japan.

Melanie and Micky were disguised as geisha visiting from another town. They looked positively radiant in their white and pink, cherry blossom-patterned kimonos. When they smiled, their tar-blackened teeth made them look elegantly toothless in the pastel lights of Lord Kaga's booming display. They twirled their parasols, fluttered their paper fans, and giggled with excitement as they watched the spectacle. Other geisha in attendance, more reserved, stared at these newcomers with cold jealousy, stabbing them with resentful eyes—as if their stares alone might make Micky and Melanie go away, or at least stop swaying so seductively.

Cup-of-Tea and Buck-Teeth sat on a nearby

boulder. Buck-Teeth marveled at the *hana-bi*, wide-eyed wonder in his easy-to-read face. At one point, Cup-of-Tea clambered down and went wandering through the crowd, feeling splendidly alone amid all the packed together "ooohing!" and "ahhhing!" people.

Cup-of-Tea smiled as he brushed past Chaz, who was singing a Def Leppard song, banging his head in the air, strumming his sheathed weapon as if it were a guitar. Chaz had fallen in with a group of Lord Kaga's samurai. They were guzzling *sake*, too, and attempting to sing along with Chaz his weird, foreign ditty. They assumed he was Chinese. Chaz and his new warrior buddies howled and hooted as the sky exploded with Kaga's emerald and blue pyrotechnics.

Cup-of-Tea also passed within a few yards of Micky and Melanie, but they missed this golden chance of meeting the master. They had kicked off their clogs and were wading knee-deep in the icy lake to get a better view. Behind them, on the bank, the furious geisha of Lord Kaga's retinue kept stabbing and stabbing them with their eyes.

Cup-of-Tea stood on the shore, not far from gyrating Micky and Melanie, his lips muttering many haiku that the world would never know. Then the final barrage of rockets orgasmed in the sky, and the townspeople and all of the *daimyo's* company let out one last, wild, collective "oooh!" It was over. Cup-of-Tea sighed.

The crowd jammed the road for the hike back to the village. Melanie and Micky climbed into their palanquin that was carried by four virile, strapping young slaves, naked to the waist. Off they trotted. Chaz stumbled, blind-drunk, with his new, hell-raising samurai friends. The merry band was fresh out of *sake*, so they started jogging, swords clattering, toward the tavern. They were nearly trampled when Lord Kaga thundered past on horseback.

Kaga was not concerned with the insignificant humanity that cluttered the dark road. He was thinking that his work here was done, that he would set aside broken hearted poem-writing and get down to the serious business of squeezing his peasants for the rice tax. His mind was so absorbed in these practical matters that, for the first time in a hundred days, he completely forgot about Lady Plum, his cruel, never-a-letter-writing mistress who languished so far away in the Shogun's capital.

No explosions now. The sky was black and brilliant with stars.

Not Looking Back

Haiku is like a karate chop, like the unrepentant thrust of a samurai's sword. There can be no hesitation, no second thoughts, no "rewrites." What pundits call haiku "revisions" are actually new poems.

For example, the night of Lord Kaga's fireworks display by the lake, Cup-of-Tea breathed out a new haiku after each bright explosion. Though many were similar, all, snowflake-like, were unique. Others in the crowd "ooohed!" and "ahhhed!"; Cup-of-Tea was busy haikuing.

Unfortunately, Buck-Teeth remembered only one of these impromptu compositions of the night. He scribbled it in his journal for posterity:

> *boom! boom! ka-boom!*
> *so many duds*
> *fireworks*

It's no accident that baseball is popular in Japan. Like karate contests or the blubbery collisions of whale-bellied sumo wrestlers, the confrontation of pitcher and batter demands split-second, absolute spontaneity: no balking, no turning back. Because if you hesitate when that pitch comes whirling at you, if you second-guess, you miss. Strike three, sucker, and the Japanese umpire behind you spits, "Out-o!"

A haiku is a Picasso-done-in-ten-seconds scribble. No time to plan, no room for regrets, no second-guessing. Swing!

And haiku is life, life is haiku.

As Shinran once said—that Buddhist patriarch who advocated sex for monks to escape the trap of trying to escape life's traps—conscious calculation is tainted by ego, spoiled like the *natto* beans that are so popular these days in Tokyo.

By the way, Melanie dined on *natto* the night of Lord Kaga's fireworks. But instead of gagging (as many do; it's an acquired taste), she licked her bowl clean and ordered her slaves to bring her more. This is just one more example of her ability to blend seamlessly among all kinds of folk: Eskimo fishermen, African villagers, and uptown New Orleans jazz musicians. All of her worldwide travels have perfectly prepared Melanie for her present visit to Old Japan. In fact, she's staying there for at least a few more chapters.

Chaz and Micky, while they enjoyed the experience, are glad to be back in New Orleans, the City Care Forgot. Melanie, though, as she always has done, has gone native.

A Puppet Show

TWO DAYS AFTER Lord Kaga's "fire-blossom" spectacle at the lake, Cup-of-Tea and Buck-Teeth walked down the hill into the village to visit an old friend of the master.

Yamakura, a reclusive puppeteer who ran a small puppet theater—the only *bunraku* theater in all that poor, culturally emaciated province—had something in common with Cup-of-Tea, for he was an artist, too. But unlike Cup-of-Tea, Yamakura felt uncomfortable in any new situation for which he was not controlling the sticks. Yamakura's lavishly costumed, two-foot-high people did not dangle from strings like their European cousins. Instead, their jointed, jerking bodies danced to the rhythm of thin black sticks that Yamakura controlled expertly from behind. In Japanese puppet theater, the puppeteer, dressed all in black, is perfectly visible behind his midget-sized cast. However, by cleverly pushing and pulling the sticks attached to arms, legs, and heads, the puppet-master vanishes behind the more colorful reality that is the play—much like God has done in the present universe.

Yamakura's two daughters, Naoko and Mika, grew up helping their father carve, paint, and dress the little people of his world. His workshop was a fantastic playground for the imaginative girls. Over time, they began to emulate their father's mute puppets, talking less and less; making all their needs known to family and friends with exquisitely choreographed, jerking body language that left no doubt as to meaning.

Their strange reliance on puppet-like charades to communicate is perhaps the reason why both sisters failed to marry in their teens or even in their twenties. One can imagine a long line of suitors sitting politely across the tea table from Mika and Naoko, trying to make sense of the spastic puppet gestures the sisters reverted to in moments of anxiety. Many would-be husbands gave up hope.

But the sisters didn't mind. They were three-dimensional, complicated female characters who didn't need men to define them.

After slurping tea politely with their host in the upstairs sitting room, Cup-of-Tea and Buck-Teeth followed Yamakura down the steep wooden stairs into the theater that constituted the first floor of the house. The audience tonight, as usual, was small. Naoko and Mika were there, a few local regulars, and one new customer who dropped a coin into Mother Yamakura's money box. That customer, blended into the shadows way in the back, was an out-of-town geisha who had attended Lord Kaga's fireworks display a few days ago and now resided at the inn. Her cool, deferential mannerisms—the impeccable way she bowed her head and flitted her fan—convinced all locals that she was pure Japanese, but we know her as Melanie.

Buck-Teeth's heart fluttered when he saw her. This was an unforeseen event, and I immediately wondered if I had done the right thing, allowing my modern-day friends into the book. Poor Buck-Teeth, smitten by a woman from another century who was just passing through his story!

Speaking of stories, the play that night told a romantic one: of lovers who commit a beautiful suicide together. The most interesting aspect of the performance, at least to Cup-of-Tea, was the costuming. Naoko and Mika had improvised a special surprise to mark the occasion of Cup-of-Tea's visit. The lead male character was dressed exactly in the same sort of earth-tone *yukata* robe that the poet always wore. Cup-of-Tea laughed with delight, although his replica's shiny-bald head made him nostalgic for yesterday's flowing, black mane. Over the course of forty wandering years, it had baked in the sun, drenched in the rain, frozen in the snow, and, finally, blown clean away.

The play's final scene, in which the Cup-of-Tea doll slit the throat of his lady doll and then, declaiming dramatic last words—by means of Yamakura's airy voice—plunged the dagger into his own heart—

When the lamps were re-lighted and the warm applause of the intimate audience subsided, Buck-Teeth stole a glance over his shoulder at Geisha Melanie. She was smiling, her blackened teeth nicely offsetting her ivory-powdered face. In terror he looked away. He felt dizzy.

As he and the master bid farewell to the Yamakuras, Buck-Teeth dared not look again at that vision of cruel perfection in her pink-and-white cherry-blossom kimono. He rushed out the door on the heels of his teacher, not looking back.

The Haiku Diary

ONCE YOU HAVE BEGUN to write haiku, you will need to start your first poetic diary.

Titling your diary is easy. On the cover write: "First Diary." Then, when all its pages are crammed with haiku and anything else you feel like scribbling in between, start a new one. Title this one, "Second Diary." And so on, on and on, until you die.

To give you an idea of what sorts of things get scribbled into a haiku diary, consider these entries from Buck-Teeth's:

***

Sixth Month. First Day. Cloudy.

Master Cup-of-Tea again held audience with Lord Kaga behind Trash House. We sat silently, watching dewdrops sparkle in the butterbur. The only sound, the deep, sad moo of a cow.

Lord Kaga shared his latest poem, dedicated like always to his Lady Plum, a strange woman. Lord Kaga loves her with all his heart, but this very love has made her lose interest.

Master Cup-of-Tea, as usual, encouraged him to try harder, saying:

> tied to a tree
> the foolish cat cries
> for love

Lord Kaga seemed not to catch the master's meaning, but plainly *he*'s the foolish cat, tied by invisible cords of passion to a mistress who cares not if he lives or dies.

***

Sixth Month. Second Day. Rain.

Master Cup-of-Tea, Lord Kaga, and I enjoyed a morning hike through the high meadows. We were caught in a cloudburst. No shelter in sight, we ran to the cover of a great white oak to wait out the storm. A miserable, shivering dog joined us.

I wrote:

>the homeless dog
>is home
>to fleas

Master Cup-of-Tea frowned. I, too, must try harder.
    The dog, whom we have named "Scruffy," followed us home.

***

Third Day. Clear.

    This morning a sad thing. A cat caught a sparrow in its mouth. The bird's frightened eyes peered at me as if begging to be saved. But the cat slid into the shadows of a thick hedge, a private place where it could continue the torture.
    I wrote:

>never more alive
>sparrow in the cat's
>mouth

I could hardly wait to share the poem with the master. First, though, Lord Kaga presented his new haiku:

>the old fart
>stacks the winter
>kindling

The master approved with a single word: "Yes." I admit, I felt jealous. And when I went on to read my haiku, Master only shook his head, sadly. Was he sad about the content, the way it was written, or both? I couldn't tell.

***

Fourth Day. Clear.

Lake Nojiriko. Lord Kaga celebrated his haiku that Master Cup-of-Tea so liked by treating the village to a wonderful fireworks display. Green and blue, the *daimyo's* favorite colors, lit the blackness again and again.

Master Cup-of-Tea spoke many haiku, but most of them I couldn't hear over the explosions of the rockets and the shouts of the crowd. This one, though, I heard in full, and it stuck in my mind:

boom! boom! ka-boom!
so many duds
fireworks

***

Sixth Month. Fifth Day. Morning shower.

With Lord Kaga gone, I feel even more pressure to shine for the master. I wrote, and shared with him,

after meeting the turtle
every rock
a suspect

...but Master Cup-of-Tea said nothing.

***

Sixth Day. Morning Rain. Afternoon Clear.

A puppet show in town.

***

Seventh Day. Breezy.

I told Master Cup-of-Tea I think I am in love with someone, but I dare not approach her. I asked: Am I doomed to play, like Lord Kaga, the "foolish cat"?

He told me this story. Once upon a time, there lived a rich old man who owned a crumbling, stinking mansion, filled with scorpions and vipers and other creatures roaming its endless shambles of rooms and corridors, seeking human flesh to devour.

This rich old man had three children who were playing games inside his crumbling mansion, amid its dangers. The children were so engrossed in their happy little games, they didn't notice the perils that surrounded them, nor the black smoke slowly filling the rooms, for the immense house was on fire.

The man, standing outside, shouted for his children to save themselves, to leave the doomed palace. But they were so addicted to playtime, words like "fire" and "danger" and "death" meant nothing to them.

Well, that rich old man came up with a clever trick. He shouted that he had new toys outside the front door, and he did: three bright carriages hitched to three different teams of animals—one to a team of goats, one to a team of deer, and the third to a team of oxen.

The kids fell for it! They came racing out of the house just seconds before it crashed to the ground. Each child climbed joyfully into his new play cart.

That was the story. I waited, expecting more. Finally, I asked Master Cup-of-Tea what the story had to do with love.

"Everything," he said.

***

Sixth Month. Eighth Day. Clear.

Today I saw her again, walking through the village in her cherry-blossom kimono, twirling her matching parasol.

My house is burning.

***

Ninth Day. Clear.

Last night the moon was full. Master Cup-of-Tea
assigned me to watch it.

I sat behind Trash House. The master came out
only once, for about two minutes; then back inside he
went. How he snores!

It took me all night, but a haiku finally came:

not a burden
moon on the bent
branches

***

Tenth Day. Muggy. Hot.

Master Cup-of-Tea shared the poem he wrote last
night:

full moon...
going out
going back in

I shared mine. Still no "Yes" on the master's lips!

White Black Green

THE VILLAGE HEADMAN found himself alone in misty woods. And to make matters worse, wolves were howling from every direction, chilling his blood.

Knee-deep in cold, white mist that slithered and snaked around the cedars, the headman caught sight of red sashes tied around their enormous trunks. So the trees were *kami-sama*, gods.

"Protect me, *kami-sama* of the cedars!" he prayed. But his prayer was mocked by a fresh volley of blood-mad howls, so near this time that he bolted, racing through the forest, kicking cold mist into swirling clouds.

Then he stopped dead in his tracks. Straight ahead in the shadows, he saw three pairs of red, glowing eyes . . . and three shaggy, hulking shapes. The howling stopped. The only sound now was a deep, three-part harmony of growls.

The headman stood frozen, praying to the *kami-sama* who towered around him. "Protect me!" he begged the tree gods once more, in a whisper.

Why was he being punished? What accounted for this sudden, bad karma? The headman's mind searched frantically for the cosmic cause of his predicament. He stood perfectly still, heart pounding, head sweating, his metaphysical question dangling, unanswered.

The headman stared with morbid fascination at the wolves' sharp, barred teeth; their strange coloration of wet, spiked-up fur. One wolf was black as soggy charcoal, another, white like dirty milk, and the third, strangest of all, was luminescent green.

"Why?!" he screamed.

In the mad rush of their attack, a black/white/green blur, the headman played a life-saving hunch. He reached his arms high over his head, looked up at the dark canopy of indifferent cedars, and began, frantically, to stroke. His body lifted! He was airborne now, rising through branches, finally breaking free into the starry, cold heavens as the wolves snapped and snarled below.

The test worked. So this *was* a dream!

He relaxed now, enjoying a leisurely night swim over strange, breast-shaped mountains. The view was breathtaking. Stars above, mountains below. He stroked higher and higher but then heard thunder. No clouds in sight, but definitely thunder. Thunder that boomed, boomed, boomed!

He woke up.

"Just a minute!" he yelled. Fists were drumming on his front door.

As he threw on his *yukata*, the village headman cursed under his breath, hating with every fiber of his being whomever it was who had interrupted his blissful flying dream. He hurled the door wide, mentally preparing to lecture this hated whomever with just the right indignant tone.

"Yes?" he hissed.

Three strangers stood on the verandah.

Nature is Not a Noun

NOW THAT THE HARVEST moon-viewing celebration is drawing near, it's time we think about Nature. If you have applied yourself carefully to these lessons, you might even be ready, and just in time, to compose a moon poem of your own. When Cup-of-Tea, Buck-Teeth, and Cup-of-Tea's three visiting poet friends gather at the lake to write haiku, you'll be right there with them, happily scribbling.

I'll save a seat in the stern of their little fishing boat for you, in case you feel up to it.

Dress warmly. On that black, bottomless lake, the wind whipping off snow-capped mountains chills to the bone. And since you're either male or female, but I don't know which, dress androgynously. Shave your head and go as a Buddhist monk or nun. Swaddled in your saffron robe and thick quilt, the full moon glinting on your smooth head, you'll look the part, as if you belong there—and you will.

Cup-of-Tea's poet friends will bring plenty of *sake* to warm your insides, or at least to trick your mind into *believing* your insides are warm. As for Buddha's precept against drinking alcohol, don't fret. Everyone will assume that you belong to Shinran's True Teaching Pure Land sect, the one that Cup-of-Tea belongs to. Shinran held that all calculating attempts to win salvation—chanting prayers, not stepping on insects, abstaining from booze, sex, and so on—only damn a person to rebirth in King Emma's deepest Hell. The desire to escape desire is the most corrupting desire of all,

Shinran insisted.

So, disguised as a monk or nun of Shinran's sect, feel free to guzzle to your heart's content and liver's distress. But be warned: *sake* is deceptively potent. And a boatload of moon-mad poets—toasting the moon, toasting each other's moon poems (that seem to get better and better, the more they drink), then toasting mothers, fathers, and even one fat, silver trout that is destined to fly out of the black depths exactly at midnight—you get the picture. Things could get out of hand. Take it easy.

If you don't feel up to haiku writing, don't force it. And don't succumb to poetic peer pressure. Just because everyone else on a wildly rocking boat is spouting ecstatic moon poems doesn't mean that you're obliged to do so.

But in case you do feel moved to babble, and to scribble what you babble, remember this: Nature is not a noun.

In Cup-of-Tea's native Japanese, the closest word to "Nature" is *jinen*, "of itself so." So when he writes,

> at the gate
> spontaneously sprouting
> spring pine

...he is marveling at how naturally, how effortlessly (literally, how "of itself-ly") the new pine shoots up out of the black, spring mud. No one outside of the pine has planned its urgent growth; nothing outside of the pine is making it. *Jinen*, spontaneously, effortlessly so, it simply is.

So if you arrive at that critical moon-gazing haiku moment, keep in mind that everything, yourself included, will be part of the picture; that nothing outside of that picture will be making the picture.

Get the picture?

If this confuses you, just sit back, pull the warm quilt snug around your shoulders, enjoy the ride, and keep your mouth shut. The others will assume you are deep in meditation, like the good nun or monk you are impersonating. They'll leave you alone. And you'll have company in your silence. Buck-Teeth will feel too intimidated by the presence of his master and famous poets from the capital to dare exhale his own haiku tonight. Besides, he'll be brooding about a certain lovely geisha in a cherry-blossom kimono—her hands, her eyes, her lips . . .

Like the wind-smacked water in the middle of that shimmering mountain lake, Buck-Teeth's mind will be way too choppy to reflect with crystal clarity the moon, the boat, the water, the poets, and you: the whole picture with nothing left out of the picture . . . and nothing outside of it making it.

To the Moon!

THE RUDELY AWAKENED headman forgot the curt speech that he had been rehearsing in his mind while throwing on his robe and stomping to the door. The three strangers standing on his verandah, leaning on pale bamboo walking sticks, were plainly the wolves of his dream.

One was dressed in funeral black, one in spotless white, and the third wore bright green from head to toe!

"Morning!" The stranger in green broke the headman's stunned silence. "I'm Mido. Well, actually, that's my bamboo-brush name—"

"Bamboo-brush name?" And before the green-robed stranger could respond, the headman gushed, "Then you must be poets. You must be here to visit our dear Cup-of-Tea, as he calls himself. See that lane leading up the hill? Straight up. Can't miss it. Good day!" He slammed the door.

The headman's heart pounded. He peeked out a window, watching his tri-colored visitors shrug their shoulders, then amble away up the road to the so-called "Trash House," clacking their sticks.

When the travelers reached the crest of the pine-shaded hill, they were warmly greeted by Cup-of-Tea, who introduced them, each in turn, to Buck-Teeth. Their names were Kuro ("Black"), Shiro ("White") and Mido (short for *midori*, "Green"). It had become fashionable in the capital, Cup-of-Tea explained, for haiku poets to adopt bamboo-brush names based on colors, and then to dress accordingly.

"Master," Buck-Teeth asked, "should I also choose a color?"

"Don't get caught up in city horse shit." Cup-of-

Tea laughed. And they all laughed, even Kuro, Shiro, and Mido—three poets caught up, body and soul, in city horse shit.

Cup-of-Tea observed, "You're just in time for the harvest moon."

"We planned it that way, Master Cup-of-Tea," Kuro said.

"Yes, wouldn't miss it!" Mido exclaimed.

Shiro, who never spoke, happily nodded.

Cup-of-Tea showed his guests the main room where they could nap on comfy, though flea-infested, quilts, for they would need plenty of rest for tonight's moon party. The three visitors, exhausted from their journey, plopped down to sleep. Cup-of-Tea and Buck-Teeth stretched out to nap, too. Soon the house filled with the snores and sighs of afternoon slumber.

Only Buck-Teeth, giddy, excited, burning with thoughts of his cherry-blossom geisha, stayed awake.

Kuro's Poetic Advice to Buck Teeth

IN THE WEEKS FOLLOWING the harvest moon party, Buck-Teeth attached himself to Kuro. The Black Poet's color was well chosen, for he constantly dwelt on the shadow side of things: on death, loss, despair, and sorrow. Because of Buck-Teeth's recent, painful failures at solving life's twin riddles, love and haiku, Kuro's grim perspective appealed to the young village poet. In dark times, dark philosophy makes perfect sense.

For his part, Kuro seized the opportunity to serve as mentor for the novice poet. Unlike Cup-of-Tea, who had yet to utter a word of literary advice to his protégé, Kuro pontificated endlessly on the dos and don'ts of haikuing. He helpfully edited Buck-Teeth's haiku,

in the dead cat's eyes
harvest
moons

. . . explaining that this original version was too optimistic, for it hinted of life in the shining eyes of the cat. Kuro removed the offending optimism:

no moonlight there—
the dead cat's
eyes

***

Life is tragedy, Buck-Teeth. Whatever you attempt to grasp, you lose, see? Are you following me? Am I making sense?

Like this geisha you pine for. You're afraid to approach her? Terrified of rejection? Go ahead, declare your love; be rejected! Believe me, you're better off without her. Good riddance!

Why? Because losing her was always, from the very beginning of time, before you even laid eyes on her, inevitable. It had to happen, whether it took days, months, or fifty years. But losing her before you had her is fortunate. This way, the other shoe's fallen, and fallen quick!

Do you follow? This is a key to our art, my young friend, the realization that all is *mujō*, temporary.

So don't love anything, anyone. Even our Master Cup-of-Tea. Don't love him. Don't feel attached to him. Nor to mother, father, or to any so-called friends you stumble upon in this life. Certainly not to me! Why? Because we are dewdrops fading to nothing! Am I making sense?

Dewdrops in a dewdrop world, Buck-Teeth, dissolving to oblivion even as I speak these words.

So why write? Because we must! Not because it will last or ultimately do any good. Don't fall into the trap of believing poetry accomplishes anything. I mean, what do you hope to do with poetry? Save the world? Earn fame and glory? Fortune?

The world's doomed, no matter what you do *or* write. And as for fame, what is it? A lot of fools who misunderstand you bandy your name about. Then later generations of still greater fools who understand you even less "immortalize" you in books. Then, still later generations of still greater fools lose all interest in you, and you're utterly forgotten.

They *will* forget you, Buck-Teeth. But if it's any consolation, they never knew you in the first place!

We're nothing but fading specks inside a fading ball of morning dew. What possible importance could anything we say to anyone have?

Still, we must record the disaster, witness the tragedy. See the dead cats! Dead cats with dead eyes everywhere!

All cats are dead; they just don't know it yet! You follow?

So do what you must, Buck-Teeth. Learn to see clearly. Get over this love business. It clouds the brain.

Am I making sense?

***

Kuro made a whole lot of sense to Buck-Teeth that autumn. So much sense, in fact, that Buck-Teeth began to believe that he had finally arrived at his long-sought solution the mysteries of love and haiku, thanks to the grim, talkative poet in black.

In a particularly euphoric moment, the morning of the year's first snowfall, Buck-Teeth summarized for Cup-of-Tea highlights of the wisdom that Kuro had imparted to him over the past weeks. He finished his account with the assertion, "Love clouds the brain!"

Cup-of-Tea, his open palms extended to catch the gently flitting-down flakes, shook his head and chuckled softly, "That Kuro!"

Back to You

I'VE BEEN SO WRAPPED UP in my private sorrows these days, crying into my Dixie beer, agreeing sadly with every depressing word that Kuro utters, commiserating wholeheartedly with the romantically hopeless and hapless Buck-Teeth—I forgot to ask how you made out the other night at the moon-viewing party.

Did you exhale a fine moon poem? Did you blend in seamlessly with that august poetic crowd, swaddled as you were in your quilt in the cozy stern of the boat, your bald head reflecting all that moonlight? And did you heed my warning about sake?

If you managed to compose a moon haiku under such battlefield conditions, I'm impressed. The boat, that night, was such a confused cacophony of both out loud and silent voices, I'd be surprised, but pleased, if you hit your first haiku home run.

Kuro's out loud voice was lecturing endlessly on the impermanence of the moon, the lake, and everything else.

Mido's out loud voice, hoarse and raucous, sang every bawdy tavern song he knew. And while he did so, he made sure, without missing a note, that each sake cup, yours included, stayed slopping-over full.

Buck-Teeth's silent voice whimpered with the pain of unrequited love.

Cup-of-Tea's voice modulated between silent and out loud. It was mostly silent, but every now and then switched to out loud, as he blurted a moon poem, then recorded it in his diary. For example, the following haiku describes something that Mido did, or, rather, *tried* to do:

> the boatman pisses
> but misses
> the real moon

And now we come to the loudest silent voice on that wildly rocking poetic vessel: Shiro's. The dressed-in-white poet had elevated silence to an art form. Kuro explained to Buck-Teeth that, according to Shiro, language corrupts haiku. A poem in its pure form exists as a nonverbal insight called a "dibbit," a flash of wordless perfection that words can never capture. For this reason, Shiro had stopped exhaling out loud poetry years ago and had settled into a complete practice of silent haiku, and, for that matter, just plain silence, every waking and dreaming moment.

You were skeptical about Shiro's silent poetry, yet, strangely, every time he was composing, everyone on the boat, including you, palpably knew it. His face softened; his eyes seemed to gaze inward. You all watched and waited, waited . . . until those inward-gazing eyes opened just a bit wider. He'd smile, then, and deeply, sigh.

"A good one, Shiro!" Cup-of-Tea exclaimed after one particularly intense dibbit.

"Let's drink to it!" Mido slurred, pouring rice wine into every cup.

You were especially moved by Shiro's wordless art. Each time his eyes announced an incipient poetic dibbit, you couldn't help but stare at his serene, moonlit face. He reminded you of Harpo, in the old Marx Brothers' movies, when the latter played the harp. Harpo's face glowed in such interludes with a mystical tranquility. Beyond the silliness of whatever wacky events spun out of control around him, Harpo, harping, radiated spiritual light. That's how Shiro looked, you thought.

Quoting Shiro's silent haiku for the purpose of this book is both easy and impossible.

Easy, because I could just do this:

But impossible, too, because I'm not sure that you, perusing the above blankness, will conjure in your heart and mind the exact same poetic dibbit that Shiro savored amid the choppy, moon-glazed water. But, then again, translation always loses something, so I suppose it will have to do.

Just as Mido was toasting Shiro's best poem of the evening, exactly at midnight, a silver trout, slippery and fat, launched itself six feet into the air, turned two back flips, and then—splash!—was gone.

"Damn!" Mido giggled.

Cup-of-Tea howled with delight. And Buck-Teeth's easy-to-read face, which up to this point had shown only lovelorn misery, shifted to register sheer amazement.

Only grim Kuro restrained himself. He commented, "That fish, a perfect image for this shitty life! We, too, thrust up into the light out of Nowhere, twist and turn uselessly; and then—so quick!—back to Nothingness we fall!"

And what did *you* think when that trout flipped around and around, slick and so alive in all that mad, dancing moonlight?

What you thought, or even *that* you thought, is unknown to me, because as I scribble these words that the Buddha dictates, I'm painfully aware that I haven't even begun to think about finding a publisher. So this untotalized text is nowhere near being word-processed, blue-penciled, galley-proofed, mass-produced, and distributed worldwide to booksellers to finally, inevitably, fall into your hands, whoever you might be: you quilt-wrapped, bald, he-she stranger in the dark stern of Cup-of-Tea's boat.

Mido's Poetic Advice to Buck Teeth

CUP-OF-TEA'S VISITING POET FRIENDS decided to stay in Kashiwabara, in Trash House, until New Year's. While Kuro seemed eager to start back for Edo, and Shiro was silent on the matter, Mido successfully persuaded them both to remain until after the Forgetting-the-Year Party. Mido loved parties, and the traditional end-of-year blast during which rice wine would flow more freely than on any other night, he hated to miss, being quite the alcoholic.

As the snow piled deeper and the poets spent more and more time indoors, huddled around the glowing coals in Cup-of-Tea's sunken hearth, Mido took it upon himself to offer Buck-Teeth some unsolicited poetic advice. Perhaps he was jealous of Kuro, whose every word Buck-Teeth latched upon like a leech to a leg. Or maybe Mido was just bored and thought to while away the last few snowbound days and evenings of the year. Whatever the reason, he held plenty of strong and unique poetic opinions, just as strong and unique as Kuro's dark philosophy and Shiro's dibbiting silence.

***

Buck-Teeth, being a poet means you've got to go out of your mind! Drinking's just one way to accomplish this. Believe me, Buck-Teeth, there are many, many ways! But warm *sake* pouring freely till dawn, haiku pals gathered 'round shouting poems, singing songs . . . well, my friend, *that's* hard to beat!

Why go out of your mind? Let's put the question another way: Why stay in your mind, your so-called "right mind?" What has your "right mind" accomplished? Happiness? Love? The perfect haiku? I think not. Have you considered the possibility, Buck-Teeth, that just maybe *you're* the source of all your troubles? More accurately, your so-called "right mind"?

Nothing great has ever been achieved by that little tyrant. Oh, yes, it can plan and measure and nail together stairways, whole temples, castles piled story upon story to the clouds, but has the "right mind" ever, since the beginning of time, created art? Never!

Has it ever let fly with cold precision an arrow shot at a fleeting bird from horseback at full gallop?

I think not!

Has the "right mind" once in all this universe of possibility dribbled an ink portrait that screams, the random is necessary, the necessary, random?

I doubt it!

And has the "right mind" ever created, by its own power, a poem for lips to babble deliciously under a full moon?

Hell, no!

Buck-Teeth, go out of your mind! Because if you stay in it, locked inside all that sniveling, careful rightness, you'll never unleash your raw voice, your true voice, the voice of your *self* beyond that scared, fictive impostor who's been posing as "Poor Little Buck-Teeth" all these years.

Poems aren't built step by step like stairways or temples, Buck-Teeth.

Are butterflies built? Are frogs planned? Do you think, like the barbarians, some ancestral god designed that black pine in front of Master Cup-of-Tea's house?

Absurd!

Nothing outside this picture is making it, Buck-Teeth.

To plan is to pretend you're outside the picture: outside the haiku, "making" the haiku. Do you think our Master Cup-of-Tea "makes" haiku? Hardly!

He's absolutely, totally, out of his mind. And there—way out there—that's where haiku just *happens*.

Tomorrow night, Buck-Teeth, at our Forgetting-the-Year Party, you'll see. Stick with me, do as I do, and—trust me—you'll get so far out of your right mind that, if you're lucky, you'll never quite get back inside it again.

Then, Buck-Teeth, you'll be a poet, whether you like it or not!

Tiny Things Like Mice

The last, short, dark days of the year were muffled in snow that piled deep and deeper around and on Trash House. The sparkling white stuff clung to the windows and blew inside through cracks in the walls, so that each morning, when the poets awoke, one by one they shook their blankets, releasing a churning, indoor blizzard.

At night the wind howled off the mountains so bitterly that Cup-of-Tea allowed Scruffy the mutt, who normally slept on the porch, to come indoors. Scruffy curled in a matted brown ball by the sputtering fire, always close to Cup-of-Tea's big, lumpy feet.

If Scruffy were human, he surely would have spent plenty of those blissful hours wondering, "What good thing have I done in a past life to deserve this good fortune? Plenty of food, a roof overhead, this wonderful charcoal fire, and a prince of a master like Cup-of-Tea!"

Of course, dogs, living as they do in the eternal now, don't bother with such meaningless speculations. One deep sigh of doggy gratitude is about as metaphysical as Scruffy ever got.

I, on the other hand, am human. Which means, my mind hardly ever focuses on the present. Right now, for example: my mind's racing nine different directions at once, while my right hand patiently scratches a blue Bic across the page. Thank Buddha, I don't have to worry about what I'm going to say!

Thanks a whole lot, Buddha, for dictating all these light, light words to me, freeing my mind to enjoy its human prerogative of racing nine directions at once. Amen.

One part of my mind is wondering what good karmic deed Scruffy might have done in an earlier life to earn his present, excellent situation as Cup-of-Tea's roommate.

Another part of my mind ponders: Should I take a bus, train, or rent a car to get to Omaha this Christmas, now that it's December 14th and I've procrastinated too long to score cheap airfare?

A third part of my mind is busy deciding how much depression I'll indulge in this womanless holiday, every winking Christmas light sure to remind me of last year when I took Natasha, my then-fiancée, north to meet the parents. Our first, and last, Noël.

And part of my mind, the fourth part, wonders whether or not this aimless text is crap. This part, where Kuro lives, constantly raises this concern.

And part of my mind, the fifth, thinks that maybe today's writing can wait. I'll hustle on down to Bourbon Street, lose myself among dizzy tourists and beer-spitting football fans, and guzzle away the rest of the afternoon at three-for-one Happy Hour in the karaoke bar. This part of my mind, where Mido revels, usually prevails.

The seventh part of my mind worries: Will my writing group complain about the pointlessness of this digression?

And yet another part, the eighth, is bored with all

this talk, talk, talk that occupies the other parts. Shiro resides in this area of consciousness that wants only to stop the NOISE.

And the ninth part of my mind, where Buck-Teeth seethes with polite rage, craves an answer to believe in.

Cup-of-Tea gives answers, plenty of them, but always indirectly, always encoded in one-breath haiku riddles. No *clear* answer presents itself to the young village poet, just more enigma piled on enigma, much like the snow piling on snow that slowly buries them all inside the master's cozy hovel.

Scruffy isn't the only new guest residing in the warm front room of Trash House. A family of quick, brown mice has moved into a crack in one of the pine walls. Every night, while Shiro, Mido, Kuro, and Cup-of-Tea heave, scratch and snore, buried in quilts in a circle around the glowing, sunken hearth; and Scruffy, lying at Cup-of-Tea's big, swaddled feet, chases dream cats . . . Buck-Teeth can't sleep. He regrets asking his father's permission to stay at Cup-of-Tea's house during the agricultural off-season, but can think of no tactful way to get out of the arrangement, at least not without appearing less than fully committed to the art of haiku. Buck-Teeth has acclimated to snoring poets and the dream-barking dog, but now *tiny* sounds keep him awake. The scritch-scritch-scritching of tiny teeth. The skit-skit-skittering of tiny feet. He tosses and turns.

Just before dawn of the year's last day, when one particularly brazen mouse skitters across the floor in the bluish first light, Buck-Teeth vents his frustration. In a frantic lunge, he stomps at the brown blur. Stomps, stomps, and misses.

Cup-of-Tea, warming pond-snail soup in a pot dangling over the hearth, witnesses Buck-Teeth's stomping and composes on the spot:

> a cold night
> the mouse escapes
> laughing!

Which brings us to the topic of today's lesson: the importance of tiny things.

Buck-Teeth's present difficulties stem from his early childhood training. Just as his practical, piss-poor parents neglected to teach him to stop, look, and listen; they also misinformed their son, when he was growing up, as to what might be worth stopping for, looking at, listening to. In fact, Buck-Teeth's parents, siblings, peers, teachers—indeed, the entire village society—had joined in a silent conspiracy to indoctrinate him (and each other, for that matter) into a false conception of what was and what wasn't important.

So where Buck-Teeth saw only a pesky vermin to be stomped, Cup-of-Tea saw the real stuff of poetry: the whole picture, nothing outside of the picture "making" it. He saw stomping Buck-Teeth and quicksilver mouse, felt the shivering cold universe all around, heard a taunting squeak, and in a heightened state of haiku awareness, captured it all in a breath.

Forgetting the Year

Buck-Teeth tried to follow Mido's advice, but did not go out of his "right mind" the night of the Forgetting-the-Year party. After three cups of warm *sake*, irresistible waves of sleepiness overcame him. By the time Mido leaned over the writing table to refill the young poet's cup, Buck-Teeth was slumped forward, head cradled in his arms, deep in a delicious slumber.

After so many nights tossing and turning to the tiny comings and goings of the mice, Buck-Teeth finally slept; would sleep all that night and much of the next day. He would wake up late on New Year's afternoon and rise a new man.

"Yes, sleep boy," Kuro said, gently pulling a quilt over him. "Enjoy the transitory pleasure, Buck-Teeth, of your dreams inside Buddha's shitty dream of this universe."

"I'll drink to that!" Mido enthused. "To Buddha's dream and every shitty thing in it!"

"*Kampai!*" the four awake poets shouted, chugging their drinks in eye-blearing samurai fashion.

"To the dog!" Cup-of-Tea raised his cup. So they drank again, this time in honor of Buddha's dream of a scruffy brown dog.

Cup-of-Tea extemporized:

"even the dog tonight
forgetting
the year."

Their end-of-year salutations, each one punctu-
ated with warm cups of *sake* tossed in unison down
four open hatches, continued into the wee hours. When
Shiro raised his cup to offer a final, touching, silent
toast, all eyes grew misty, for the poets realized that
tomorrow morning the three students and their be-
loved master would part.

On wobbly legs, they stumbled to the frozen rear
of the house, where the walls were glazed with thick
ice. Cup-of-Tea flung open the rickety back door for
the night's, and year's, final pissing, it being too cold
and the snow too deep to visit the privy. Buddha's uni-
verse was a still, frozen dream dazzling with snow be-
low and sparkling stars above. The poets each at-
tempted to piddle one last haiku of the year in the snow
bank by the door.

Cup-of-Tea scribbled his poem first, but ran out
of fuel halfway:

> Heaven's River
> of stars . . .

Then Kuro composed, also incompletely:

> breaking through ice . . .

But Shiro's dibbit was complete, by Shiro's standards.
Deep into the snow bank he wrote:

Finally, Mido, his bursting-full bladder equal to the task, mustered just enough piddle to complete:

farewell! farewell!
pissed
in a bank of snow

After their snow-scribbling, the four poets returned to the warm front room, rolled into quilts for the year's last sleep, and slept.

At that precise moment across rumpled snow- and ice-crusted mountains far to the east, in the Shogun's frozen capital, Lady Plum was gliding from room to room, barefoot, in a blood-red kimono, her face a hard, white mask of deception. From room to empty room, and empty inside, ghostly, she glided.

In Kashiwabara, the snow-buried Trash House resumed its nightly chorus of sleep sighs, snores, muffled dream-barking at dream cats, and underneath all those large sounds, the tiny skittering of quick, tiny feet. The charcoals in the hearth glowed bright orange, happily sputtered.

And the year was forgotten.

PART TWO

Buck Teeth Wakes Up

WHEN BUCK-TEETH'S SLEEP-CRUSTED EYES finally, slowly pried themselves open on the year's first short day, Trash House was empty and still. The only sounds were shuffling footsteps and muffled voices on the other side of the partition wall. Buck-Teeth recognized old Satsu's brittle, "Nyat-nyat-nyat!" tone, which meant she was nagging her son, poor Senroku. Buck-Teeth sighed.

On Cup-of-Tea's half of the cozy farmhouse, not a creature was stirring, not even a mouse. The entire family cuddled asleep in their snug apartment in the wall.

On the writing table that had served as his head-rest for the past fifteen hours, Buck-Teeth found a haiku scrawled on a scrap of rice paper in Master Cup-of-Tea's unmistakable, blotchy, chaotic scribble. It read:

trusting in Buddha

the year

ends

Buck-Teeth hurried through the freezing back of the house to perform a pressing biological task. He shoved the back door open with a sense of true emergency, as his first act of the new year was already underway, with or without his conscious participation.

In the snow bank by the door, just as Buck-Teeth was aiming his spontaneity, he discovered a surprise: the piss-scribbled poems and half-poems of Mido, Shiro, Kuro, and Master Cup-of-Tea. Buck-Teeth smiled, feeling enormously relieved, relaxed, and satisfied, standing alone in Buddha's vast, icy, overcast dream. Without premeditation, he finished the unfinished works in the snow.

Kuro's incomplete haiku of

breaking through ice

...Buck-Teeth completed with:

crack!
in the outhouse

And Master Cup-of-Tea's unfinished haiku,

Heaven's River
of stars

...Buck-Teeth finished with:

in my soup

Yawning, stretching, shivering, his breath puffing clouds, Buck-Teeth turned to go back indoors. Then it hit him. His easy-to-read face—if only someone had been there to read it!—beamed sheer joy. Without planning it or expecting it to happen, Buck-Teeth on the first day of the New Year had become a new man.

He was a poet!

Simply Trust

BUCK-TEETH'S HAIKU epiphany, as epiphanies must, took him by surprise. I was also shocked by the suddenness of his poetic breakthrough. I had assumed that this would not happen before Cup-of-Tea gave his young disciple much more instruction. I had imagined that Buck-Teeth's final graduation to the status of true poet wouldn't happen for dozens of chapters, if at all. But this unforeseen turn of events teaches me once again not to second-guess the Buddha from Beyond who dictates this text, urging my scratchy, blue Bic on and on across pages of this slowly mounding-up Mount Fuji of paper on my kitchen table. I should keep my opinions to myself as to where all this is heading, and leave the pen-driving to the Buddha, while I gaze out the bus window, enjoying my human birthright of letting thoughts wander. The Buddha has his job to do; I have mine.

By the way, I won't be taking the bus to Nebraska, after all. I was able to book a cheap flight even at this late date, so I'll soon be flying to my *furu sato* ("native village") of Omaha. I'll keep you posted.

But enough about me. How are *you* doing? Are you feeling pretty good about getting this far into the text, or are you still asking yourself, like last year's Buck-Teeth, what's the damn point? Did you happen to catch the lesson that the Buddha cleverly tucked into the previous chapter? Hint: it lay nestled inside Cup-of-Tea's gift poem to Buck-Teeth.

trusting in Buddha
the year
ends

"Trusting in Buddha" is exactly what Buck-Teeth, his creative instrument firmly in hand, accomplished as he stood on his master's frozen back porch on the year's first day. Memories flooded his heart-mind, then, as he realized with grateful tears that he had been wrong in believing that Cup-of-Tea had not breathed a word on how to write haiku. On the contrary, the master had been exhaling many such words for the better part of a year, hidden in crafty parables. For example:

in Buddha trusting
blossoms trickle
down

and...

trusting
they scatter to nothing
dewdrops

"If only I had listened!" Buck-Teeth exclaimed, his breath puffing clouds.

If you, too, "simply trust" (*tada tanome*), your mouth might also one day pop open like a New Year's gift and haiku come pouring out. To trust is to follow the Old Fool himself, the Buddhist patriarch Shinran who shirked rules and commandments. For if you *try* to become enlightened, you've damned yourself to hell's stew pots for the pious. If you *try* to write haiku, you've damned yourself to suffer the sleepless misery of last year's Buck-Teeth. If you *try* to fall in love—etc.

Simply trust. That's what Buck-Teeth did, astride that glittering snow bank riddled with sunken, yellow ciphers.

The Inevitable

THE INEVITABLE CONSEQUENCE of waking up one day and discovering that you are a *bona fide* haiku poet, as Buck-Teeth has done, is to take to the road on that all-important first literary journey.

When Cup-of-Tea returned home and discovered two perfectly, spontaneously completed haiku piddled in the snow behind his house, he knew right away that Buck-Teeth would be leaving. The boy's poetic break-through delighted and saddened the master. It also frankly shocked him. Like me, Cup-of-Tea had assumed it would take a long time for Buck-Teeth to "get it"; he had so much to unlearn! We were both wrong. The Buddha works in mysterious ways.

After Buck-Teeth left, so soon after the departure of Shiro, Kuro, and Mido, Cup-of-Tea's half of the divided house felt a hollow kind of empty. Even the mice skittered a bit more nervously in all that new silence.

But it *was* inevitable. Cup-of-Tea himself had wandered off, in his late twenties, after his master Chikua died. To everyone's amazement, Chikua had named Cup-of-Tea, a bumpkin from the hills, as his successor to lead the school. Cup-of-Tea had obeyed his master's dying wish at first, but his heart wasn't in it. The road called.

He left Edo on his own first, inevitable, haiku journey, abandoning Chikua's school. He crisscrossed the provinces, scribbling haiku in a weather-beaten diary, dressed like a Buddhist *unsui* ("Cloud-Water") wanderer. Like clouds that can't stop drifting, like water that can't stop flowing, the *unsui* poet-priests of Old Japan saw travel as a way of life and a path to enlightenment. They were not "on vacation" or "sight seeing" but rather wandered for a sublime purpose: to realize Buddha's salvation, the Pure Land, here and now.

You might be thinking: Didn't Shinran warn that anyone who seeks salvation is doomed not to find it?

So true. Enlightenment is nowhere to be found. You can roam hither and yon your whole life, clacking your bamboo walking stick on endless, winding roads— and not attain the Buddha's peace. You can't find enlightenment by wandering; you can't find it by staying at home. But still, you're better off hitting the road, because, as Cloud-Water wanderers soon discover, on the road enlightenment has a better chance of finding *you*!

The reason is simple. A traveler experiences Kuro's favorite word, *mujō*: transience. Here today, gone tomorrow. Cherished notions of permanence slip fast away when "home" is that night's inn. On the road, one gets so used to saying, "Farewell!" to all persons and things, eventually, "Farewell" replaces "Hello." Coming upon Mount Fuji for the first time, the traveler says, "Farewell, Fuji!"—knowing full well that this awesome splendor will eventually be just a memory. Or, waving to a stranger approaching in a thick mist, the Cloud-Water rambler whispers, "Farewell, stranger!"—for that stranger too, like Fuji, will soon enough be gone.

One morning, after all this farewelling, wanderers glimpse their own ragged reflections in mirrors, see nothing but stark impermanence, and exclaim, cheerfully, "Farewell, me!"

Saying goodbye to yourself is a baby step into Buddha's Paradise.

Heading South

FOR HIS FIRST POETIC JOURNEY, Buck-Teeth planned to visit Edo, meet with his new friends, Shiro, Mido, and Kuro, and then go on to Kyoto, the old capital, and points south.

He needed a change of scene. If prophets are not recognized in their hometowns, this goes double for poets. His dirt-poor parents couldn't understand why their clever son devoted so much time and effort to scribbling words that did not put food on the table. Buck-Teeth's father was especially disappointed. He had hoped that his son's shoulder-rubbing with Lord Kaga would at least lead to a position in the *daimyo's* retinue. But Buck-Teeth showed no interest in exploiting his acquaintance with Kaga. *I've raised a fool!* his father thought.

Buck-Teeth's father shook his head sadly, gazing out the window at the snow-covered radish field on the hill, withered leaves trembling in the First Month wind. Buck-Teeth's silhouette, as he crouched low to peer at something small, broke his father's heart.

"From now on, the boy's got to work. Full-time!" he announced to his wife.

The next morning, at dawn, Buck-Teeth left.

Buck-Teeth's father's bewilderment is not unfamiliar to me. Just the other day, Christmas Day, after my family's gift extravaganza in the basement, turkey feast in the dining room, and sleepy stupor in the den, I decided to slip into the kitchen to see if the Buddha might not inspire me to add a page or two more to this wandering text.

The old blue Bic began scratching.

After a while, my father came in.

"What's that you're working on?" he asked.

My father, a retired mechanical engineer, is the consummate practical man. How could I explain to him that I was devoting so much precious life energy to an endless, directionless, and seemingly purposeless book?

I stammered, "It's something I'm writing," and handed him Chapter 1, titled, "Once Upon A Time."

He sat at the table sipping decaf and reading, intense furrows creasing his forehead.

Part of me felt excited, proud even, that he was paying the same scrupulous attention to my words that he might to a broken washing machine or a rusted-shut fuse box. But a larger part shivered with fear.

He finished, removed his reading glasses, and looked up with a puzzled expression.

Finally, he spoke.

"Why don't you write about Nixon?" he asked. "There's never too many books about Nixon!"

***

Buck-Teeth clacked his walking stick on the Shogun's snaking mountain road. A north wind blew him along, like a frail ghost in Buddha's cold, vast dream. He trudged south toward Nakajima, his lunch stop, but his mind was in a puppet theater. Physically, he walked alone on the Shogun's ice-slicked road, but mentally, he basked in the black-toothed smile of a geisha he could not forget, despite what Kuro had taught him.

Season's in Life's Year

BEFORE WE REJOIN BUCK-TEETH on the road, I should say something about the Haiku Seasons of Life.

A proper haiku always has a *kigo*, a "season word" that grounds it in the great cycle of life: New Year's, Spring, Summer, Autumn, Winter—Birth, Childhood, Maturity, Old Age, Death. And, rolling, rolling—another new year with Birth, Childhood, and so on. On and on.

A *kigo* can be obvious or subtle. An obvious kigo plainly announces the poem's season, as in the following example, a haiku I wrote on the plane coming home from Omaha:

silent night, holy night

three

at the bar

The first phrase, "silent night, holy night," is from a Christmas song, and so it evokes the winter season. And the next poem in my hip-pocket pad, a composition of just the other day, is also seasonally obvious:

my New Year's resolution

buy

toilet paper

Often, though, a haiku's season is only hinted at. Take the moon, for instance. The moon shines all year 'round, but when mentioned in haiku, unless a different season is specified, it invariably is autumn's harvest moon. The following example from Buck-Teeth's journal,

> not a burden
> moon on the bent
> branches

...thus refers to a harvest moon, in the shorthand of haiku.

The coincidental season, the time of year during which a haiku happens to be written, is not important. What matters is its poetic season, the Season of Life to which its content belongs. Hence, Lord Kaga's haiku,

> the old fart
> stacks the winter
> kindling

...is a winter piece despite the fact that we know it was composed in Sixth Month.

Nagasaki

BUCK-TEETH, MIDO, AND KURO reached Nagasaki in a sleet storm. Shiro had decided not to accompany the others on their southern journey, but remained in his fishing hut under the willows on the bank of Sumida River, thinking poems and waiting for spring.

Mido now thought of the Poet in White, for Buck-Teeth's long silence reminded him of Shiro. "You've been about as talkative as you-know-who," he teased. But Buck-Teeth said nothing.

The trio passed through the gate of the city and started down a dismal street.

"Ever since the miracle," Kuro observed in a tone that expected no response.

"Lunch," Buck-Teeth muttered.

"Oh, you're hungry?" Mido was encouraged by Buck-Teeth's first word in many, many miles. "I was beginning to think you were lost to us forever, dibbiting! Well, welcome back, stranger! Yes, let's do find a decent meal in this miserable town."

They sloshed through the miserable town, bent under umbrella-hats of woven bamboo, the sleet drumming their portable roofs with a dreary monotony. The Poet in Green, Mido; the Poet in Black, Kuro; and Buck-Teeth, who wore no particular color, plodded through Buddha's cold, gray dream.

"Sign of life!" Mido smelled cooking smoke.

Why bother? Buck-Teeth thought. *The book's over. The inspiration's dried up. This whole scene, destined for the drawer.*

But he kept this gloomy thought to himself. Such depressing ideas had darkened his heart-mind for days, ever since sighting the mysterious geisha in the cherry-blossom kimono. He had spotted her on the road to Kyoto. She had grinned at him for a moment, then had looked past him, as if at a point a thousand miles away.

"Excuse me, miss," he had said.

But the old blues line, "If it weren't for bad luck, I'd have no luck at all," fit Buck-Teeth perfectly in this situation. Just when he had finally worked up the nerve to talk to his ladylove, Melanie became bored with Old Japan, and left the book.

Not a word of goodbye. Not even a wink. She faded into thin air, to nothingness, on her way back to New Orleans, to the future, to her two slobbering dogs and jazz musician boyfriend.

Buck-Teeth's depression oozed darkly. He stared at his boots mechanically stomping the slush that appeared the color and consistency of snot. But there was *something* to look forward to at least: lunch. It was *soba*, judging by the aroma carried in the wafting smoke. Definitely *soba*. Definitely lunch.

Soon they were out of the sleet, huddled over steaming bowls of buckwheat noodles. The tiny noodle shop was toasty warm.

Kuro and Mido grabbed their chopsticks, lifted their bowls, and commenced slurping.

Buck-Teeth sighed and followed suit. Before long, he had to admit to himself: *But this* soba *does taste fine! Even if the scene served no purpose in furthering plot or teaching lessons in the art of haiku, the thick, hearty noodles swimming in a broth topped with raw pheasant eggs were exactly hitting the spot. The shop was cozy, warm, and dry. It was good to be alive, if only for another page.*

"Now *that's* the spirit!" Mido exclaimed, noticing the faint smile on Buck-Teeth's face.

"We die soon enough anyway," Kuro philosophized

in a gentle tone, as if he'd heard and understood every word of Buck-Teeth's tormented inner monologue of the past several days.

"How did you know?" Buck-Teeth gasped into his *soba* bowl, afraid to meet Kuro's eyes.

"Your face, Buck-Teeth. Didn't anyone ever tell you? It's *damn* easy to read!"

The Barbarian

BY THE TIME HE FINISHED his bowl of noodles, lifting it to his lips to suck the last delicious drop, Buck-Teeth was cured of all suicidal thoughts. In fact, never again in his long, poetically productive life would he come as close to ending it as he had in the past several days. Happily, he would live to see his eightieth year, when death would greet him like an old friend, prompting him to jot the very last words of his diary:

seen it all, done it all
and now
forgetting

Kuro was glad. He had sensed Buck-Teeth's despair ever since the miracle on the road to Kyoto, when that strange girl had strangely vanished, and he felt it deepen the day they crossed over to Kyūshū island by ferryboat. Kuro knew that Buck-Teeth was nothing more than a temporary illusion inside Buddha's dream of a universe, but he couldn't bear the thought of parting with this particular illusion, not yet, not before his time. Despite all his lecturing for one to avoid attachments, Kuro had grown quite attached to the young poet and, though he would not admit it even to himself, he loved Buck-Teeth.

"Look, a barbarian!" Mido whispered loudly, nodding toward a huge, dripping figure standing in the doorway.

"Are you open?" the barbarian asked the shopkeeper in slow but passable Japanese.

"I've heard of such things," Kuro said in a low voice. "But I thought the Shogun had closed Nagasaki's port."

The barbarian looked exotic with his bushy red beard, thick, curving fingernails, and billowing, black breeches. He threw off his great blue overcoat and matching wide-brimmed hat, shook water from both with a flourish, and deposited himself at the next table, elbow-close to Mido.

"*Soba*!" the barbarian demanded.

"Barbarian," Mido addressed him in a friendly tone, "would you like to join us in some *sake*?"

The barbarian nodded.

"*Sake*!" Mido bellowed at the shopkeeper.

The barbarian, named Hans, turned out to be an agreeable fellow, willing and eager to answer all the poets' questions about strange lands across the deep, blue ocean. This particular barbarian, they discovered, was pious, a follower of Jesus. He told them that he worshipped the God-man who died on a cross and then rose from the dead as proof of his divinity.

Buck-Teeth's interest was piqued. "My master, Cup-of-Tea, told me of your cult. Once he showed me in one of his diaries the account of his own journey to this district, where he came upon an ancient statue of your sect. He wrote:

"Great Japan—
overgrown with weeds
Jesus-Buddha."

"It's a sad history," the barbarian sighed. "You probably don't realize what happened here, not a mile from where we sit, not so many years ago. Twenty-six believers of Jesus were crucified by the samurai. Those twenty-six martyrs followed the Bishop of Rome, while I, on the other hand, am a..." Hans the barbarian fumbled for a word that did not yet exist in Japanese. "Well, let's just say that I follow Jesus but not the Bishop of Rome."

"And your Saint Jesus, is he a Buddha, as my master writes, or a *kami-sama*?" Buck-Teeth was trying hard to make sense of the barbarian's odd faith.

"He's the only son of the one and only true *kami-sama*. In fact, he is one in being with the great *kami-sama*."

"So he's his own father?" Buck-Teeth asked.

"Yes. And he died for your sins."

"*My* sins?"

"Yes. So you can go to Heaven one day, and not burn forever in Hell."

Buck-Teeth's mind flashed to his own Paradise and

Hell: Paradise being a vision of a pretty geisha in a cherry-blossom kimono. Hell: the moment when that same vision, that pretty geisha, vanished.

"But Heaven and Hell," Buck-Teeth explained, "exist already for me, both of them."

"No, my son. When you die, your soul goes *forever* to either Heaven or Hell. Only those who believe in and follow Lord Jesus go to Heaven. The rest all burn."

Kuro grinned, shaking his head. "As if!"

Hans failed to see humor in what he had said. His fat, freckled face wrinkled into a frown.

"Forgive me, barbarian," the Poet in Black said, "but I find your wishful thinking precious. As if we were real in the first place, to suffer or enjoy any condition for an eternity!"

Kuro went on to "witness" to the barbarian, as he loved to do, how we are but dewdrops fading inside Buddha's fading dream of a universe; how, too soon, every one of us dissolves back to the Big Fat Zero from whence we came.

"I'm sorry you think that," Hans said, after Kuro finished. "I'm sorry for *you*."

"And I'm sorry for *you*, pinning hope on a future that can't exist," Kuro replied good-naturedly.

"Well, we aren't going to settle this here, today," Mido observed, refilling all four *sake* cups for another round. "So let's drink to *this* moment, here and now, whatever the future brings!"

Everyone, even Hans the barbarian, joined in Mido's toast, drinking, "To now, *kampai!*" And the three Buddhist poets, who believed that they were dreams, and the Christian merchant, who believed that he wasn't, at least agreed on one thing: it was good to be alive in that cozy, warm noodle shop in Old Nagasaki.

Lunch had been good. Buck-Teeth was back among the living.

The Writing Group Contemplates Suicide

LAST THURSDAY AFTERNOON, I could hardly wait to share my recent chapters with the group. I was especially excited about the scene in the Nagasaki noodle shop. Watching the copy machine spew copies of my latest installment, I was relieved to be writing again, and effortlessly.

Micky didn't have anything for us that day, her character Micky temporarily stuck at the Bulgarian border. Chaz brought only a paragraph, and since Melanie's true-life vignettes were always short and sweet, I felt that this session would be, after a long dry spell, *my* day to shine.

We settled in our circle of chairs in Micky's spacious corner office, where all our meetings were held, and began with Chaz's paragraph. One of his monsters attacked and mutilated a furious bull named Hammerstomp. I put in my two cents, hoping to end it quickly and move on, but the others talked endlessly about minutiae, such as whether the blood should spurt or gush. Micky, who favored gushing, and Melanie, spurting, acted as if Chaz were paying them by the hour! I glanced at my pocket watch, frustrated.

Finally the issue was settled—Hammerstomp's blood "sprayed"—and it was on to Melanie's latest true-life story, this one about a guy pulling up next to her at a red light and yelling to ask what radio station she was listening to. Micky and Chaz yammered on and on about "adding more description."

"I can't see it, smell it, taste it," Micky complained.

"Be more specific," Chaz suggested, vaguely.

Melanie thanked them, and, at last, my moment of writing group glory was at hand. I distributed my copies and then recited my recent chapters out loud, loving the sound of Buddha's words flowing trippingly off my tongue.

"...Lunch had been good. Buck-Teeth was back among the living." I laid the pages on Micky's coffee table cluttered with foreign paperbacks. I looked up with a modest smile, waiting for the accolades that were sure to come: a verbal barrage of long-stemmed roses.

A long pause.

"A barbarian in a book about haiku?" Chaz frowned.

"Shades of Flaubert!" Micky said, pronouncing Flaubert with an extreme French accent.

Melanie, smiling like Mona Lisa, said nothing.

Then Micky changed the subject, I *think*: "I wonder if we all committed suicide now, would it make national news?"

The rest of the meeting was devoted to this grave question. Everybody, even Mona Lisa Melanie, gushed opinions.

An old Buddhist proverb warns, the nearer we approach Truth, the fiercer grow the demons and guardian monsters whose job it is to drive us off the path. Biking home after the meeting, rolling under the dark Carrollton Avenue overpass, it hit me: my writing group, through no fault of its own, had become my own impeding demon, a fierce guardian monster intent on driving me down the mountainside, now that the story was telling itself again.

Or maybe it was just a case of the group outliving its usefulness. Pedaling down the avenue, I realized how alone in this world we are, we separate masks of the Buddha: Micky, Melanie, Chaz...

You, me, Buck-Teeth...

From Buck Teeth's Diary Later That Year

ELEVENTH MONTH. Third Day. Morning Snow.

We have stopped at Norida, a village nestled among hills looking like an earth-dragon's burly shoulders. The arms connected to these shoulders plunge down into a silver bay. A universe of snow surrounds: white hills, white sky. I think of Shiro this morning, our Poet in White. The blankness of this place, I'm sure he would love.

> an ink-black crow
> in the dead
> of white

Our own crow in this washed-out world, Kuro, took

me aside this morning and whispered gravely that he thinks Mido will not leave this place. He has established himself as a fixture in the tavern, where he talks endlessly with locals—fishermen and tea-girls. Already he never pays for his drinks. So many want to fill Mido's cup, hear Mido's songs, laugh at Mido's jokes. But Mido, our Poet in Green, is fading.

I say to Kuro, "Maybe he'll bounce back, like he has before." But I doubt my words.

Last night, dangerous men stepped into the tavern, two swaggering samurai. Mido woke from his stupor.

"You, samurai!" he shouted. "Come drink with us!"

Kuro gestured for Mido to shush. I whispered to him, "I don't think that's a good idea."

But again he shouted, slurring his words together, "Samurai-I'm-talking-to-you!"

The samurai watched Mido, Kuro, and me with narrowed eyes, as if choosing targets. They slowly approached.

"Sit!" Mido said, meeting their stares. "I wish to talk to you." Then to the serving girl he commanded, "Bring sake!"

The samurai, with tight, grim smiles, sat.

"So, tell me," Mido said. "How many men have you killed?"

I held my breath. Kuro sat still as a black shadow against the wall. But Mido simply would not shut up.

"We are poets," he explained. "We write. You, my friends, are samurai." He lifted his cup while the girl was still refilling it. "You kill, don't you?"

"Yes," the fatter one grunted. "We kill."

***

"I love war," the clean-cut one, the one wearing plastic-rimmed glasses, said. "It's what I know."

"We should have gone into Baghdad," his buddy, scraggly-haired with a wispy, brown Fu Manchu, complained.

It was St. Patrick's Day. The tavern we sat in, Polly's on Toulouse, was packed with a raucous crowd gulping dollar pitchers of green beer. The jukebox, its speakers dangling from the rafters, vomited heavy metal mayhem.

"What's that book?" the clean-cut one asked me.

"Just something I'm reading." I handed him my battered Puffin paperback translation of *Buck-Teeth's Diary*.

"Any good?" he asked.

"I think so."

The one with the Fu Manchu, a Vietnam vet in a brown leather motorcycle jacket, steered the conversation back to the original topic that the two had been loudly discussing, war.

"I was two years in country." He picked up his green brew and took a swig. In the space between his index finger and thumb, I noticed a red gecko lizard tattoo.

He belched and continued. "I was a specialist. I mined rivers. First sign of Charlie in the water, I threw a switch, and boom. But for months, nothing. All we did was hang around and smoke opium. You ever smoke opium?" he asked me.

I shook my head, no.

The place was loud and crowded. I leaned on the bar and cupped a hand to an ear to hear his tale.

***

"A rebellion in the north. A glorious slaughter."

"Peasants." The thinner samurai grinned. "Every five years or so, especially after a drought, the fools rise against the rice tax. Keeps *us* busy."

"So you're mercenaries?" Kuro asked.

"We have no lord," the fatter one said. "Except money."

They both laughed.

***

"I was on sentry duty, high as a kite, smoking that opium, tossing the control box into the air, one hand to the other. Everything looking like slow motion.

"Down on the bridge, a convoy was rolling. So I think to myself: Why not just set it off? See what happens."

"You *didn't*!" The clean-cut one was loving the story, his eyes gleaming.

"It was righteous! Two walls of jungle water rising and rising—a hundred feet, two hundred feet. On both sides of the bridge, funky water rising in slow-frigging-motion. But then it stopped and came down—splash!—on the convoy. And I'm too numb even to laugh. Seems funny, but then I get paranoid. How am I gonna cover my ass?"

"What did you do?" I asked.

"I decided I'd swear I didn't do it. Charlie must've set off the charges, I'll say. Some such shit. But I don't need a story."

"Why not?" his companion asked.

"Dude, there was a hand."

"What?"

"A human hand. It dropped with the water and the fish, landed in one of the trucks. Someone *was* in the river."

A fresh wave of revelers pushed into the bar, college babes with fluffy manes of blow-dried hair. The warriors took notice. The clean-cut one handed me back my copy of *Buck-Teeth's Diary* and proceeded to flirt.

I opened the book and continued reading.

***

Their playful way with the tavern women surprised me. The fatter one, in between toasts, folded a scrap of paper with delicate care into a crane. When he was finished, he gave it to a small, pale tea-girl who wore a blue kimono decorated with plovers and waves.

She giggled, delighted, and led him away, upstairs.

Mido grinned stupidly.

I wrote:

the killer's hands
fold a paper
crane

Kuro and I left the tavern at midnight. Mido, as usual, remained to sleep in his corner. His soul will not allow him to leave, he told us. If he dies there, he said, his ghost will not go thirsty.

Buck Teeth Visits New Orleans Disguised as a Tourist

YOU AND MY WRITING GROUP comrades visited Old Japan, so in the interest of fairness, a native of that place and era should tour modern New Orleans. Buck-Teeth is the logical choice, since he has recently committed himself to a life of Cloud-Water wandering. Allowing him to visit my adopted city, as my writing group experienced Lord Kaga's fireworks display at the lake and you moon-viewed in Cup-of-Tea's boat, seems right and just.

And so it shall be.

***

Buck-Teeth arrived in New Orleans just this morning, disguised as a Japanese tourist. He materialized in azalea bushes near one of the old cannons in a corner of Jackson Square. The 38 millimeter camera with zoom lens slung around his neck was pure prop. No film was in it, because Buck-Teeth intended to take *his* snap-shots poetically, with pen and paper, in haiku.

It was a splendid March morning, this morning. The sun peeked out of clouds for the first time in a week. Buck-Teeth's easy-to-read face beamed with toothy anticipation. Instead of his regular bamboo brush, rice paper, ink, and ink-stone, today he carried, tucked in his shirt pocket's pocket-protector, a small spiral pad and a blue Bic roller-pen.

Consulting his foldout guide map, he took his bearings, then walked straight ahead, past the white cathedral, up Pirates' Alley. Soon he was standing on world-famous Bourbon Street.

"Hey man, I bet I know where you got dem shoes!"

"Are you talking to me?" Buck-Teeth asked, proud of his instant knowledge of English.

"I bet you ten dollars I can name the street, city, and state where you got dem shoes!"

Buck-Teeth considered the proposition. Since he had just materialized out of azalea bushes in Jackson Square, he was confident that the fellow wearing the baseball cap backwards couldn't possibly know where he "got" his shoes. Buck-Teeth himself did not know.

"OK," he said, after deciding it was a no-lose bet. "But you'll never guess."

"You got 'em on your feet, on Bourbon Street, in N'Awlins, Louisiana!"

Now the man dropped to one knee, smeared some clear goop on Buck-Teeth's brand-new Reeboks, and proceeded to buff them with a rag. He held up an open palm.

"Gimme twenty."

"But our bet was for ten!"

"Ten for the rhyme, ten for the shine!"

Buck-Teeth paid up. He didn't know it, but he had just fallen for one of the French Quarter's oldest hustles, guaranteed to work on haiku poets from Old Japan and newly arrived teachers from Nebraska.

Buck-Teeth strolled down Bourbon Street, gawking into sex-shop windows where inflated plastic women and men gawked back. He marveled at the whips and chains, but could not fathom the purpose of the dildos and nipple clamps.

Roaming up and down the strip twice, he decided to enter one of its landmark establishments. Its name, glowing seductively in gold neon over the door, was "Dreamland." Inside was dark with smoky, chilled air. Buck-Teeth had to stand still for a minute to let his eyes adjust. The throbbing beat of hip-hop music rattled his bones. A hand cupped his elbow firmly.

"Bar or booth?" a woman asked.

Buck-Teeth chose the bar. He stumbled into the seat that his scantily clad escort guided him to. He ordered a beer, and before he had time to focus on the erotic bumping and grinding above him on the stage, a husky voice tickled his right ear. "You want company?"

The woman, a buxom blonde in a red dress, settled into the chair next to him. A barmaid appeared, asking, "Would you like to buy this lovely lady a drink?"

"Why not?" Buck-Teeth said. He paid for his tiny glass of beer, the "lovely lady's" cocktail, and left a tip—fifteen dollars already spent, and he hadn't even been in Dreamland a whole minute yet.

(Go ahead, Buck-Teeth, enjoy yourself. If you run out of cash, I'll just write you more!)

The song ended. The dancer clicked down from the stage in tottering high heels and very little else. She came straight to Buck-Teeth and leaned over him, her breasts bobbing.

"Would you like to tip me for my dance?" she purred.

He did so.

When Buck-Teeth finally stumbled, drunk, out of Dreamland, it was dark outside. At the door, he was thanked lavishly by Amber and Chocolate, the two women who had "double-teamed" him all afternoon in a booth: Buck-Teeth the bologna in a voluptuous human sandwich. The other dancers shook his hand, too: Karen, Louise, J.T., and Kiki. Buck-Teeth tipped everyone generously, including the doorman in the cowboy hat. They were all delighted that their visitor from Japan had made a slow day a payday.

"Tell your friends from that Kashi-wa-who's-it place they're welcome here any time!" Kiki, the last one to shake the village poet's hand, said.

Buck-Teeth wrote this haiku upon leaving Dreamland:

somebody's little sister
Bourbon Street
stripper

I made sure to pick a full moon night for Buck-Teeth's visit to our age, for such moons have a way of making the creative juices of haiku poets gush. As the Quarter grew darker, louder, and more crowded, Buck-Teeth scribbled several haiku in the little spiral pad that I had provided him with, for example:

> the good little moon
> has
> a halo

> faint pink lips
> where someone kissed
> the window

> kissing moon goodnight
> a gentle
> drunk

Just at midnight, I caught a glimpse of Buck-Teeth in the flesh. I was sitting at my regular corner table in my favorite karaoke bar, watching two Canadians on stage roaring, "Born to be Wild!" For just an instant, my eyes caught Buck-Teeth's. He stood on the crowded sidewalk outside, peering into the place through the window behind the stage. I saw him plainly between the legs of one of the large Canadians. He was lean, pale, and much taller than I had pictured him. When his dark, urgent eyes caught mine, they widened with astonishment.

Then, poof!—he vanished.

More From Buck Teeth's Diary

ELEVENTH MONTH. 15th Day. Overcast.

Mido quit drinking. Kuro and I could hardly believe our eyes, this morning, to find our skeletal friend sitting upright on his bench in the tavern, sipping green tea. We joined him for bowls of spicy snails and rice. He gobbled and smacked his lips so loudly and with such gusto, Kuro dared to ask, "No *sake* today?"

Mido shook his head, no.

He threw down his chopsticks and lifted the bowl to his lips. He tossed back his head, swallowing the dregs.

"It's strange, Kuro," he said. "But when I woke this morning, I realized right away, my first thought, I'd lost my taste for it."

We stared at him, disbelieving.

"I'm through with *sake*," he said, smiling strangely.

"Then we'll leave this place!"

"Yes, Buck-Teeth. We'll leave this hellhole."

Mido stood, his frail, green-robed figure trembling. He hooked his thin arms over our shoulders, and we walked him out of the tavern into the gray, winter morning.

He said, "I suppose I'll need to find some other way to get out of my right mind, won't I? Now that *sake* tastes like liquid crap!"

"Don't worry about it," Kuro said. "Being in your right mind was never a problem with you, and shouldn't be now."

I felt elated. Mido quitting *sake*! Mido out of the tavern! His soul no longer thirsty, our journey could continue. Where would we go, next?

I was thinking these thoughts, supporting our friend's light, light body, his feet shuffling, then not shuffling at all. They just dragged in the snow, plowing furrows, letting Kuro and me do all the work as we walked him to the inn.

When we got to the door, his wide-open eyes told us he was dead.

Shiro's Advice to Buck Teeth

When he had first met Cup-of-Tea's tri-colored disciples back in his native village, Buck-Teeth had been bowled over by Kuro's dour poetics and impressed by Mido's ecstatic poetics, but never had quite gotten around to explore seriously the quiet, empty poetics of Shiro. Now that Buck-Teeth was traveling his own haiku road, experiencing life in its myriad, mysterious deepnesses, he decided he could use all the poetic help he could get. Hence, he visited the White Poet's shanty in the willows just a few weeks after Mido's cremation.

Over steaming green tea, the interview began.

"Master Cup-of-Tea taught me, Shiro, by action more than words, life is haiku; haiku is life. And there's no single way of looking at either. So if both are un-fathomable, ultimately, are we not doomed always, only, to scratch at surfaces?"

Shiro sat there.

"Not really 'doomed'. That's a negative way of putting it. But the more I travel, the more I see, everything—without and within—is becoming so darn *slippery*. It's getting hard, Shiro, to blurt the poetry that once blurted itself. Does this mean I should follow *you*, just shut up and dibbit?"

Shiro sat there.

"But I want to *say* something! I doubt I have it in me to follow your pure path. How do I reach the middle ground, between saying too much and silence?"

***

I sit here.

On my regular stool, in present time, reading my well-worn Puffin paperback translation of *Buck-Teeth's Diary*. Buck-Teeth's account of his visit with Shiro strikes home, for I, too, am feeling poetically blocked today. My eyes wander the club, a Friday afternoon at 4:00 p.m. Happy Hour, and I wonder: Can a one-breath poem do justice to *this*?

***

"So much goes on, Shiro, and it all interconnects! Everything with everything else! And every which way I look, I see *too* much, it seems. My head hurts; my thoughts skim surfaces. I'm tongue-tied."

Shiro sat there.

***

Floating clusters of blue, orange, and red balloons bob over the tables. The M.C. croons "Crocodile Rock." At the bar to my right, hunched into a book, an old woman reads. Two bored waitresses in red T-shirts stare into space, waiting for tourists to stumble in. Beyond the open windows behind the stage, Bourbon Street shimmers in the glare of the afternoon sun. A fat man puffing on a black cigar cruises by in a power wheelchair. A pigeon dive-bombs a box of trash. "Gutter punks" with pierced faces lounge on the sidewalk. A toothless wino attempts a wobbly tap-dance. So many sights and sounds in this one, here/now moment—way too many for a single haiku! And just as I perceive it, *this* moment glides inexorably into the next, a new configuration, a new reality—like a bumped kaleidoscope.

***

"I keep thinking, Shiro, when I want to write, there's something that needs to be said. I worry that I'm missing it, and end up saying nothing."

Shiro sat there.

"At Mido's funeral, my heart-mind ached; I was bursting full with feelings and memories, but I wrote nothing."

Shiro sat there.

***

I sit here.

I nod my head. *Yes, Buck-Teeth. I know where you're coming from. Attachment's no good. We're both attached to our words, our poetry, expecting something from it, of it, though Kuro warned us about this. Our very love for the product, a pretty haiku, kills it in the bud before it can exist.*

***

Shiro sat there.

***

I stare into my beer. I wonder, do all poets reach the point where they see *too* much and then write nothing? What should I do, then? Go to the source, perhaps? Visit Japan? I do have some money saved up...

***

Shiro sat there.
Shiro sat there.
Shiro sat there.
Buck-Teeth wrote, and I'm reading:

scratching the snowy
surface of things
mouse

BUCK-TEETH WANDERED the western mountains till the spirit gradually tugged him homeward toward his native village. Noticing the direction he was veering, he decided to make the most of it and visit his parents and his haiku mentor, Cup-of-Tea.

It was early spring, but a light, powdered-sugar snow dusted the road the morning he reached Zenkōji, the major temple of Buck-Teeth's province. He decided to stop for a quick visit before hiking the last fifteen-or-so steep miles to the village.

At the edge of the temple precincts, he paused at a stand of plum trees, feeling a wave of nostalgia. His father and he had a picnic here, years ago, under these blossoms. Buck-Teeth continued, passing through the great gate with its sneering gargoyles. Vendors hawked incense sticks, candied plums, and prayer beads. Up the wide promenade to the main temple hall, Buck-Teeth walked.

Beggars appraised his shabby poet's clothes with quick, professional glances and didn't bother holding out their little boxes.

At the entrance to the main temple, Buck-Teeth kicked off his straw clogs, adding them to a long queue of footwear. He stepped barefoot into the cool, dark interior. All was exactly as he remembered.

To the right of the golden image of the Buddha, pilgrims lined up at a small passageway. Buck-Teeth knew where it led: down a staircase to a pitch-dark tunnel, which passed directly under the Buddha.

How many, he wondered, would be saved this morning?

He remembered a New Year's Day long ago, when his father took him down that same dark passageway. As they descended, his father had explained that somewhere in the absolute blackness below, at a point exactly underneath the golden Buddha, a hand-sized hole had been hewn into the wall by ancient monks. Anyone who groped through the darkness and happened to thrust his or her hand into that secret niche would be reborn without fail in Buddha's Pure Land.

Centuries after Buck-Teeth's visit, the pious still shuffle through the dark tunnel, but nowadays a friendly tour guide pinpoints the lucky hole with her pocket flashlight, so that every single pilgrim, in our modern age, is saved.

***

He is not afraid as he clambers down the dungeon-dark steps below the temple. He is at the end of the pilgrim line, and his father already has vanished below, in shadows. It is cool in Buddha's narrow, dark world. With no one behind him, he takes his time, believing absolutely what his father told him on their way to Zenkōji this morning.

"Rebirth in the Pure Land, son, is a lucky thing. It's like this. Imagine a blind turtle swimming somewhere in the ocean. Once every century, he rises to take another hundred year's breath, then back to the deep he dives. Meanwhile, drifting aimlessly on the surface of this ocean is a single plank of wood with a hole cut in its center. Rebirth in Buddha's Paradise, son, is as lucky as that blind turtle rising to the surface for his once-a-century breath, and poking his snout through the hole in that aimlessly drifting plank. But be patient; it *will*, eventually, happen!"

Buck-Teeth takes his father's words to heart. His right hand, which he cannot see, he fancies is the snout of that sea turtle, and his slender wrist, its neck. The hand-sized hole in Buddha's cave, hidden in blackness, is that plank, he imagines, drifting on the waves, beckoning him to Paradise. How he longs to make that lucky insertion, and tell his father afterwards that he, Buck-Teeth, just ten years old, did it!

Now at the bottom of the staircase, he enters the corridor, touching the cold stone wall lightly, below waist level, as his father had instructed him to do. He walks slowly, slowly—until it feels just right.

When he thinks he has gone far enough, Buck-Teeth stops. He can see nothing, and hears only his own breathing, his own heart pounding, as he raises his hand, holds it shoulder high, and jabs it toward the wall.

***

Later, as they trudged along the Shogun's snaking road back to the village, his father asked if he had made the lucky fit. Buck-Teeth hid his bruised fingers in his coat, but his downcast face told the whole, sad story of religious failure.

"Father, were you lucky?"

"Of course. Every time!"

The sect founder of Zenkōji, Shinran, rejected celibacy as a prerequisite to achieving the Buddha's peace. Shinran believed that all intentional actions to achieve salvation are corrupted by selfish desire. If you remain celibate all your life thinking this will guarantee rebirth in Buddha's Paradise, this same selfish thought—winning rebirth for *you*—damns you to King Emma's deepest Hell, Shinran said.

If you go down into the darkness trying to hit the mark, you've already missed it, Shinran said.

Salvation is a lucky thing, brought about wholly by the Buddha from Beyond. It has nothing to do with good deeds or following rules or diet or chanting or with any intended, ego-tainted effort, said Shinran.

Buck-Teeth realized now, after all these years, that his father was a liar of the highest degree, one who believed in and would defend to the death his lies, his illusions...bless his greedy little heart. But stage-center in the Great Hall sat the Buddha: a fat, grinning simpleton. And all of Buck-Teeth's haiku pals, the living and the dead, were wonderful fools. He smiled, happy to be human in that moment.

He left the main hall, retrieved his clogs, and picked a spot to sit not far from the smoldering incense cauldron. He crossed his legs, opened his satchel, dampened his ink stone, ground in a bit of fragrant ink, dipped his bamboo brush, looked up, looked down, and scribbled in his tattered book:

in the pink dusk
with pimples—
face of the moon

Buck Teeth's Homecoming

BUCK-TEETH HAD A STRANGE HOMECOMING.

The first strange thing about it occurred on the Shogun's highway just before its last steep curve into the village. A boy whom Buck-Teeth vaguely recognized rounded the bend, toting a bag. When the boy looked up from his daydream and saw Buck-Teeth, he gasped and dropped the bag, spilling rice onto the road. He spun around and took off running back up the hill and out of sight.

Buck-Teeth wondered what it meant. The boy would surely catch trouble, leaving precious grain on the road, times being hard. Buck-Teeth guarded the spill for a spell, but finally decided that the boy was not returning. He shrugged his shoulders and continued up the hill.

The second strange thing about Buck-Teeth's strange homecoming utterly tested his sense of reality. Just as he reached Kashiwabara's outskirts, he heard shouts. Then, thundering around the curve came a dozen samurai in full battle gear, their long and short swords clattering.

Buck-Teeth hopped into the slush-filled ditch, threw down his satchel and stick, and groveled as decorum required. He waited for the troops to pass.

They didn't.

Instead, they came to a halt around him. Hands lifted Buck-Teeth as if he were light as rice paper. On the shoulders of two stocky samurai he rode into the village.

"It's Buck-Teeth!"

"He's here!"

The entire population of Kashiwabara lined the narrow street, cheering. Buck-Teeth's easy-to-read face expressed utter amazement.

"Welcome home, son!"

He could hardly believe his eyes. Was that really his father, the piss-poor farmer, squatting on the village headman's verandah between the grinning headman and great Lord Kaga himself?

Lord Kaga's samurai lifted Buck-Teeth up to the verandah, depositing him on a cushion.

"You needn't look so surprised, Buck-Teeth. It isn't every day a village welcomes back one of its own," Lord Kaga said.

Buck-Teeth was speechless.

"Do you not remember *Willow Moon*?" his father asked.

Buck-Teeth remembered but was shocked to hear his father speak these words. How could this illiterate farmer, who never in his life had left his home province, possibly know about *Willow Moon*? It was the title of a book that he, Mido, and Kuro had thrown together one night at a poem party in Edo. Shiro had hosted the party at his shack in the willows, under a First Month moon. They had passed around rice paper and rice wine, scribbling and drinking, drinking and scribbling. Up to this moment, Buck-Teeth hadn't given it a second thought.

A child of five stood on the straw-packed street below and recited:

> "a moonlit gourmet—
> cat
> in the garbage."

Buck-Teeth was stunned. *He* had written that haiku! How did a child come to know it by heart?

"You're famous, son!" his father exclaimed, then went on to explain that handwritten copies of *Willow Moon* had circulated last summer in the capital, becoming all the rage. Lord Kaga, recognizing Buck-Teeth's name and with fond memories of their audiences behind Cup-of-Tea's Trash House, decided to have the manuscript printed with illustrations of birds, flowers, and frogs—and a preface written by the *daimyo* himself. In Edo, the Shogun's poem-drunk capital, it had become a sensational hit, a haiku bestseller.

In honor of the book's fabulous success, his father said, beaming, Lord Kaga had most generously exempted their family from that year's rice tax.

Demand for his son's haiku had grown so great, the proud father added, a sequel had already come out, a slender volume titled, *Invisible Cat*. Thumbing quickly through the copy his father thrust into his hands, Buck-Teeth had an eerie feeling. It was as if he *had* written all these crisp, off-the-cuff poems that he now was seeing for the first time. Each haiku in the sequel sounded exactly like something he *might* have written. Some knockoff artist in the capital had done splendid work indeed, imitating a style that Buck-Teeth himself still somewhat lacked confidence in.

Food was hauled onto the verandah and laid before them on large, lacquered trays, a bubbling, aromatic feast of high country delicacies. Musicians played a festive song with flutes and drums. Dancing girls, wearing Lord Kaga's favorite colors of emerald and blue, pranced in the street.

Suddenly, Buck-Teeth sensed a palpable absence. Something or someone was missing from the scene...

"Where's Master Cup-of-Tea?" he asked.

The Renga Party

REMEMBER HOW I TOLD YOU that writing haiku is a social activity, like sex or bridge or singing karaoke tunes on Bourbon Street? I should have mentioned then—but, better late than never; I'll mention now—the *renga* party.

Chaz of my writing group threw a party for me before I left for Japan, a farewell dinner. He arranged to meet me and two other co-workers at an uptown sushi restaurant. I suggested that we write a *renga* together, since I was about to visit haiku's homeland.

Renga is linked verse, poem after poem written by

poets taking turns. In our case, we passed around a yellow legal pad, each of us inventing a haiku that responded and added to what was written before.

We had a blast. Four friends gobbling sea urchins and smelt eggs, guzzling Kirin beer from giant bottles, belching and laughing and composing haiku with dizzying speed...Mido would have loved it.

Let me start at the beginning. When I arrived at the restaurant, Chaz already had claimed a table and was working on an enormous bottle of beer. I joined him, and the petite Japanese waitress handed me a hot, wet towel. I covered my face with it—a warm, pleasurable feeling. When I lifted it...

***

"Buck-Teeth! Pay attention!" It was Kuro.

"What?"

"You dozed off again. It's your turn."

Buck-Teeth looked down. Sure enough, rice paper, ink, and brush sat beneath him on the little table.

"Ah, moon and *sake*," Mido sighed. "A powerful combination!"

Shiro, in white, sat like an iron-spined ghost against a willow's craggy trunk.

Buck-Teeth read the page. Mido had begun the *renga* with:

> willow, moon
> and a river...
> of sake!

After which, Kuro had written:

> tabby cat on moon patrol
> stepping light

And now it was Buck-Teeth's turn.

***

When Paul and Bert arrived, Bert suggested that we make up pen names for the *renga*.

"That's how they did it in Old Japan," he explained. "It was a way for poets to divorce themselves from the constraints of ego."

Bert had spent a whole year studying in Japan and obviously intended, ego or not, to run this thing.

Our waitress approached. "Would you like something to drink?"

Paul, red-bearded and soft-spoken, ordered the same huge-sized beer as Chaz and I were guzzling. Bert, showing off his Japanese, gushed, "*O-sake, kudasai!*"

"*Hai*," she answered, then left.

"*Sake*," Bert announced, "tonight my name is *Sake*!"

Chaz rolled his eyes. He seemed impatient to get the *renga* underway, tapping the legal pad with his pen.

"Is a pseudonym necessary?" Paul asked.

"Na," I said. "Just use one if you want to."

Bert frowned.

Chaz uncapped his pen. "I'll start," he said.

"Wait!" Bert, I mean *Sake*, urged. "First, we'll need a

theme!"

Chaz and I exchanged glances. When Chaz had suggested having sushi in honor of my trip, I right away had thought of inviting Bert. A big-boned, studious fellow with thick, black-rimmed glasses, Bert was a new teacher at the college where I taught literature, Chaz taught psychology, and Paul trained teachers. Bert was an economist.

"May I suggest," he said now, "dark water as our theme? The levee and the river are just a stone's throw from here."

"Fine with me," Paul said.

"Whatever!" Chaz said, and started writing.

"Wait! Wait!" *Sake* raised his hand. "We haven't agreed on structure! Now, a *real renga* starts with a haiku of five-seven-five syllables, followed by a shorter verse, which—"

I interrupted. "We don't have time for all that. Can't we just adopt one simple rule: that whatever we write should be short enough to say in one breath?"

Chaz agreed. Paul nodded. Majority ruled. The game began.

When Chaz passed the pad to me after scratching down his opening haiku, he whispered, "Nazis followed orders, too!"

***

Buck-Teeth dipped the horse-hair tip of his brush into the ink, glanced up at the moon for inspiration, and let poetry flow:

a moonlit gourmet—
cat
in the garbage

Mido found *his* inspiration in his *sake* cup, swigging from it and then writing:

backyard moon
mosquitoes rush the poem

Kuro responded, poetically, on a somber note:

no one gets out alive
blossom
world

***

Chaz's first haiku contained the same gory imagery that fills almost every page of his thriller-in-progress:

red moon
like a blood-ball
in darkness

I added, quickly:

over a black river
it hangs

Bert, in the guise of Sake, now took his turn. He counted five-seven-five syllables on his big fingers and, slowly, wrote:

> the river's darkness
> silvered with rocking moonbeams
> fills me with regret

He passed the pad to Paul, whose haiku, after Bert/Sake's laboriously composed one, was re-freshingly spontaneous:

> a full moon again
> horny
> again

Everyone around the table, even Bert, cheered.

Me in Japan

I WAS FINALLY IN JAPAN, and it felt like home.

I gawked out the open window of the train, a lumbering, squealing local from Narita to Tokyo, and everything that I laid eyes on—stark green patches of rice fields, squiggly characters worming down a bill-board, the jet-black hair on every head of every person in sight—seemed familiar, seemed right. I was, it seemed, exactly where I had always belonged.

Maybe I was a haiku poet from Buck-Teeth's day, reincarnated and now, at long last, returning to the motherland...? I smiled. Even if it wasn't true, it was a delightful thought.

I was being noticed in Japan as a strange one. Unlike most foreigners who streak from Narita airport to Tokyo on the express train or else in the air-conditioned, whisper-quiet comfort of a limo-bus, I had opted to ride a slow, stop-go-stop local train that screeched into, and lurched out of, every Podunk station. I was the only foreigner in a car chockfull of Japanese people. From what I could tell, I was the only foreigner on the train.

This word, "foreigner" (gaijin), I heard stage-whispered more than once behind my back. But I didn't feel like an outsider, though I definitely stood out in my frayed black T-shirt, raggedy blue jeans, and large, blue-and-white Reeboks. Unlike most tourists, I had no hotel reservation, knew no one in the whole country, had no plans, no itinerary, no idea where I would end up this night (and it was getting dusk) or where I would sleep, or where I would go tomorrow.

Back in New Orleans, when I had applied for the visa, I had been instructed to write on the official form the name and address of my hotel in Japan, or of a Japanese citizen with whom I would be staying, as if traveling without such arrangement made in advance was unthinkable. How times had changed on the home islands since Buck-Teeth's day! I solved this dilemma by flipping through my guidebook and listing the first hotel that my eyes fell upon as my Japanese address.

Like Buck-Teeth when he traveled, which was most of his life, no one in the entire universe that is Buddha's dream was expecting me tonight. No paper lantern—or electric light, for that matter—glowed for me in a friendly little window anywhere.

I was perfectly alone, happily so.

After a transfer amid the chaos of one Tokyo station, then a whooshing subway ride to another, this one called Ikebukuro, I entered a bright, underground mall. I flowed with the surging masses and was spat out of the concrete-and-glass bowels of the earth, up an escalator, like Jonah from the fish.

Muggy air and gushing neon. Cars. People. Ten thousand sounds.

I had arrived. I was home. I was in Ikebukuro.

I was lost.

Buck Teeth Gets Regrounded

Buck-Teeth was eager to climb the path to Trash House. His homecoming party on the village main street was past dead. His parents had excused themselves hours ago. Tired, gray, twin souls, they told him to enjoy himself and stay out as late as he liked, that his old room would be ready for him when he got home.

Lord Kaga, though a partymeister to rival even the dearly departed Mido, stifled a yawn. His attendants, whose job it was to hold aloft the emerald and blue globe lanterns attached to long bamboo poles, were fighting sleep. Their lights bobbed and swayed. Green and blue-tinted moths circled in mad flurries.

Kaga's flutists were out of breath and splitting tones. Thick-armed drummers thumped their skins listlessly. *Samisen* girls plucked their twanging strings with plectrums held in numb, white fingers.

"Thank you, Lord Kaga, for everything," Buck-Teeth said. "But I must be going."

A musician within earshot smiled gratefully.

"Very well." The *daimyo* clapped Buck-Teeth on the shoulder. "In the morning, come see me at the inn. We have business to discuss."

Buck-Teeth climbed the steep, crooked path that led up the hill to his master's ramshackle abode. It felt good to be alone among the shadowy pines after hours of suffering the village's and Kaga's greedy attention. A farm dog barked in the distance. An owl hooted. Other than these sounds, and the shuffling of his own weary feet, blessèd silence poured into Buck-Teeth's ears. By the time he reached the house at the crest of the hill, his strange homecoming in the village below felt like an absurd dream. Still, he thought, it would be wise to see the master now, even if it meant waking him. Cup-of-Tea's no-horse shit attitude would be just the thing to help Buck-Teeth get re-grounded in reality. He banged a fist on the soot-blackened door. It creaked open.

"May I help you?" a woman asked.

Buck-Teeth was stunned. Who was this beautiful, heavy-lidded female opening his master's door in the middle of the night?

"I, er, uh...I'm Buck-Teeth. I'm very sorry to call so late. I stopped by, you see, wondering if perhaps Master Cup-of-Tea might be awake?"

She smiled. "I know you. My husband's finest student."

Buck-Teeth couldn't help but blush. Had Cup-of-Tea *really* said that about him, that he was his "finest student"?

This question, though, was quickly replaced by another in his mind.

Did she say "husband"?

The Puffin Translation

THE SUMMER I WENT TO JAPAN, I couldn't yet read much Japanese, so everything I knew about Buck-Teeth and the art of haiku was filtered through translation, specifically, through my tattered, Puffin paperback translation of *Buck-Teeth's Diary*. Like all translations, Puffin's is flawed. Its language is far less musical than the original, and it bombards the trained eye with glaring errors, I've been told. However, as translations go, it's better than most.

I relied religiously on my banged-up Puffin, now that I was in Tokyo, attempting to retrace Buck-Teeth's erratic footsteps. The text, though flawed, was my one link to the Japan of old: the Japan of Buck-Teeth, Mido, Kuro, Shiro, and Cup-of-Tea. It was a Japan which, I realized now, standing amid the neon-lit bustle of Ikebukuro, was forever gone.

Luckily, the Puffin translator accurately expressed in English Buck-Teeth's feeling of rootlessness, his lightness, the way his heart fluttered each time he hit the road on a new, aimless journey. Standing in the drizzle, my soggy blue backpack slung over a shoulder, I felt exactly the way Buck-Teeth felt, according to his *Diary*, the night of his homecoming, centuries ago in Old Japan.

***

He didn't say goodbye to his parents. He couldn't face them. And as for his appointment with Lord Kaga tomorrow morning, he would break it. Buck-Teeth guessed that Kaga's "business to discuss" would involve a loss of freedom; that the *daimyo* would offer—and once offered, impossible to refuse—a court appointment. Buck-Teeth, already sick of fame after several hours of it, yearned for the open road.

Nothing was left for him in his hick village nestled in the mountains. It was a moonless night and the crickets chirped madly when Buck-Teeth took his final, tearful leave of his haiku mentor, Cup-of-Tea, and Cup-of-Tea's new bride, the lovely, heavy-lidded Kiku. At first, Buck-Teeth had considered going home and spending the night, what was left of it. But when he reached his parents' farmhouse—this one night in a thousand, a little lamp glowing in a window just for him—his feet kept moving. He shrugged his shoulders and obeyed them.

And vanished.

***

The Puffin translator correctly portrays how Buck-Teeth never had the least idea as to his destination whenever his feet compelled him, as they did that night, onto a new journey. This thought consoled me now, since I had arrived in Ikebukuro, one of Tokyo's busiest districts, without a hotel reservation. It was nine in the evening, and I soon discovered that "proper" hotels had finished registering guests at six. Their dark front offices posted "CLOSED" signs in the windows. It was one Japanese character that I figured out all by myself.

I wandered into a rain-streaked, garish red-light district of hostess bars and porno theaters. In this neighborhood, the so-called "love hotels" were just beginning to turn on their electric signs.

I entered one such establishment; its purple neon *hoteru* sign had beckoned from midway up a crooked alley. The lobby looked drab and ordinary by the naked light bulb that dangled from the ceiling. Its yellow light cast deep, wavy patterns—like sedimentary rock—in the desk clerk's face. I recited lines to her from my guide book's "Hotel Dialogue," which, miraculously, worked. The old woman produced an enormous key, and led me up a dark flight of rickety stairs. She unlocked a door, opened it, and clicked on the lights.

Everything within was cotton candy pink, from the lampshades on the little pink tables to the heart-shaped pillows on the big, pink, heart-shaped bed. Curvaceous nudes cavorted with Cupids and Pans in lurid, Western-style paintings that hung on pink walls. The woman chattered something at me that I could not understand, gave me a strange, inquiring look, and then left me alone.

"Look out, Buck-Teeth," I said, "I'm right behind you!"

To my delight, the half-sized pink refrigerator was fully stocked with my favorite Japanese beer.

Crashing Symbols

INEVITABLY THE MIND PLAYS SYMBOLS. But if you allow the control-mad, analytical part of your mind to seize a moment, especially a haiku moment, beware. Such moments, like trembling gazelles when the lioness is near, die quickly. The analytical part of your mind licks its chops with glee, declaring to itself and to anyone who will listen, with smug satisfaction, "I figured it out!"

But you haven't.

Consider this example, one of Cup-of-Tea's best-loved haiku:

katatsuburi
soro soro nobore
Fuji no yama

In one of my undergraduate classes at the Jesuit college in Omaha, I read J. D. Salinger's novel, *Franny and Zooey*. Somewhere in that book, this poem by Cup-of-Tea appears in translation. Here's my own version:

little snail
inch by inch, climb
Mount Fuji!

To illustrate the wrong approach to symbolism, let's imagine that this scene of a snail creeping up the great mountain stands for something, and let's try to figure out what this "something" might be.

"It's obvious!" Intellect roars. "It's a parable of persistence, the snail symbolizing how a person, slowly, slowly climbs to the 'impossible' goal. End of story." Jowls dripping with blood, Intellect moves on to stalk new prey, perhaps the *New York Times* Sunday crossword puzzle.

This rush to judgment has utterly closed down the possibility of coaxing further meaning from Cup-of-Tea's moment. All has been defined, confined, mastered, killed. In the future, when the thinker of this thought stumbles upon the poem again, on page or in memory, he or she will not *see* it. The haiku will be encountered as a puzzle already solved: "Oh, *that*; that's the perseverance thing!"

But haiku should be approached in a less grasping way. Instead of pouncing, we should emulate the little hero of the poem and inch slowly, slowly *toward* meaning. This keeps the haiku, and the moment, ever alive, as they should be, and, really, are.

When I first read this haiku, back at the Jesuit college, I visualized a snail scaling the real Mount Fuji, which I knew from pictures to be vast and snow-capped. But years later, when I visited Japan, I was told by a haiku enthusiast on the bullet train to Kyoto that the poem really describes a pseudo-Fuji, a man-made imitation-Fuji, a mere hill in a temple garden. If so, then the snail has a much less imposing task than in my original thought. However, both images work. It is Fuji; it isn't Fuji. Let all images that pop into your mind, be. When you close your eyes and imagine the scene, right now, what do *you* see?

little snail
inch by inch, climb
Mount Fuji!

Keep your lioness of intellect on a short choke chain! Don't let her attack the visionary moment head-on. Force her to circle and circle the gazelle that is the poem. See it move, kick, blink, tremble, and, constantly, change.

Play with symbols, but do not grasp them. Pick them up, one by one, like pebbles in a stream; consider one, toss it back, pick up another.

Try this pebble: the snail is the poet Cup-of-Tea on his haiku journey through life.

Or this: the snail is you, reader, and Cup-of-Tea in the moment gently pokes fun at how you, we, plod along on your, our, absurd quest to understand this very poem.

Or try this: the snail's just the snail. That's all.

Or: the snail is Buddha, which makes Fuji the universe and its peak Supreme Enlightenment.

Or: Fuji's just Fuji.

Or: Fuji's an imitation Fuji in a temple garden, as I was told in Japan, so the poem depicts how people are misled by false assumptions, the snail a poor fool clinging to a huge misconception.

Or: the mountain in the haiku is each of us, our true, immense Self, which makes the snail our creeping, one-thought-at-a-time, intellect, what Mido called the "right mind."

Or: there is no mountain, as Zen priests like to tease.

Or: the snail is climbing Cup-of-Tea's *idea* of a mountain.

And so on, on and on.

See what I mean? The haiku remains alive, bountifully yielding meanings simply because we respect the depths of the moment. Don't try nailing just one interpretation onto a moment! This is a lesson I myself am learning as this text spits onto paper from the tips of countless generations of blue Bics. In earlier chapters, I began to suspect that the Buddha might be dictating dark allegories of my own life. For example, I would have sworn that Lady Plum, cold-hearted mistress in a blood-red kimono swishing through her icy palace, "stood for" my ex-fiancée, Natasha. That would make me the "old fart," Lord Kaga! But only for as long as I hold this bizarre thought in my brain, which isn't long at all.

Dredging symbolic meanings from the depths of any moment, any haiku, is fun and perhaps inevitable. Just don't get attached, once you pick up a pebbly truth. Toss it back right away. Don't cling.

From My Japan Journal

JUNE 5TH. Tokyo. Cloudy.

First full day in Tokyo. Woke up in a "love hotel" somewhere in the Ikebukuro district. My room completely pink and funky, but I love it. So much so, I paid the old woman at the desk for another night. She shot me a strange look. "Who is this *gaijin* staying in a love hotel with no lover?" she must wonder.

> the old woman's mouth
> painted on
> crooked

Already Japanese is seeping into my brain. At a crosswalk near Ikebukuro station, I heard a young mother tell her child, "*Aoi!*" when the light turned green, and I actually understood her. *Aoi* means "blue." I wonder if in ancient times blue and green were one color...? In any case, I felt tremendously self-satisfied to understand what *o-kaasan* (Mother) had said.

hold Mommy's hand!
the light turns
blue

Visited bookstores and purchased every haiku book that the friendly clerks handed me. Who knows? Maybe someday I'll even learn to read them. My most prized acquisition of the morning was a fat, green, imitation leather-bound copy of Buck-Teeth's haiku diary, *Deba no nikki*. Flipping it open as I stood in the Maruzen book shop, I felt butterflies in my stomach. My eyes ran lovingly over its pages of black, squiggly characters in neat, vertical rows. I thought, with rever- ence and excitement, *These are Buck-Teeth's words!*

five thousand characters!
I can read
"mountain"

My afternoon was disappointing. I trekked around the city, by subway and on foot, looking for signs of the Old Japan of my idols. First, I tried to locate the site of Shiro's fishing hut in the willow grove on the banks of Sumida River. I searched several blocks of glitzy, high-rise office buildings, but found no trace of a hut—and not a willow in sight.

Undaunted, I hunted next for Lord Kaga's mansion. I knew from the map on the inside cover of my Puffin translation that this was located somewhere near the end of the Sakurada Moat. All I found there, though, was a police station. I shrugged my shoulders and moved on.

I had saved the best for last: Buck-Teeth's final hermitage, a place beyond the old city that long since has been engulfed by urban sprawl—the place to which Buck-Teeth, as an old man, came down from his beloved mountains to die. I collated my Puffin map with a subway guide and soon was underway. I rode the Tozai line to the correct stop and rushed out of the station.

My jaw dropped.

A European-style *castle* loomed on the horizon! Atop dozens of spires, bright flags flapped in the wind. Camera-toting tourists stood in a long line.

All this for Buck-Teeth! I marveled, feeling a surge of pride for the village poet who made good. But then I noticed a sign in English.

Buck-Teeth's hermitage was no more: "Welcome to Tokyo Disneyland."

June 10th. Higashi-Koganei. Rain.

Today I am exploring Higashi-Koganei, a comfortable, laid-back town west of Tokyo. To escape a morning drizzle, I ducked into a little place called "Tommy's Rock Box."

Here I sit nibbling seaweed salad and slurping tea. It's dark in Tommy's, but a gooseneck reading lamp casts a pale circle on the table, just enough light for me to add to this journal that I've sadly neglected these past several days.

Tommy's is intimate. Nothing more than a cubicle of black walls, a few tables, and a giant, high-density screen showing music videos. Across a low counter is a closet-sized kitchen/DJ booth. The sound system is state of the art. Bass booms so deeply, the walls shiver.

Jimi Hendrix rocks.

Negotiating seaweed from plate to mouth with chopsticks is a challenge, but I forego the fork that the waiter/DJ has provided, obviously due to my *gaijin* status. As a matter of pride, I force my fumbling fingers to the task.

> offered a fork
> again—I feel
> foreign

A pretty young woman named Yumi was just now puzzling over a *Far-Side* book. She knows a bit of English, but not nearly enough to get the jokes. I tried explaining to her the humor of Moby Dick stuffed in a taxicab, but failed miserably. The language barrier was too great for that, but not too great to prevent us from making a date. Tomorrow, we will visit a nearby mountain she told me about: Takao-san.

June 11th. Mount Takao. Clear and warm.

Yumi met me at the Higashi-Koganei *eki*, where we caught the next west-going train to the end of the line, Takao-san-Guchi. She wore a fuzzy pink sweater, blue jeans, and hiking boots.

On the train, I attempted to explain to her, in my faltering Japanese, my deep love for haiku, especially for that written by the great Buck-Teeth. She, however, showed little interest. Yumi is a child of the new Japan, much more into Madonna and the Spice Girls than the traditional arts of her native land.

At one point, she referred to me as *kanemochi*, "rich." I tried to assure her that, where I come from, teachers are not well paid and certainly not "rich." But she was not dissuaded.

"*Kimi wa kanemochi darō*," she insisted. I *must* be rich, to visit Japan on such a whimsical mission, re-tracing the footsteps of bygone poets!

We rode the train to Takao-san-Guchi. Deep green foothills, looming mountain, a happy stream rushing through the town. There, we transferred to a cable train that crawled up the side of the mountain to a lofty gift shop/restaurant with a breathtaking view. It wasn't, however, the summit. We tramped up a path, stopping now and then to admire the great, towering cedars—"*sugi*," Yumi called them. The oldest and most magnificent ones had bright red sashes tied around their trunks.

"*Kami-sama*," she explained. Which meant, these ancient trees were *kami*, gods.

waterfall smash, crash!
then down the canyon
laughing

We reached the summit and visited a Buddhist temple, its buildings scattered among steep, wooded cliffs. Yumi bought me a souvenir key chain with a red-faced, long-nosed *tengu*, a grimacing goblin that she said was good luck. I bought her an appointment book handmade by the monks.

As we walked back down the trail holding hands, she made it known, with simple Japanese and simpler English, that she would very much like to visit me in America someday, and she even suggested that I send her a ticket.

"But I'm not *kanemochi*!" I protested.

Yumi just squeezed my hand and smiled.

PART THREE

Kaga the Hermit

THAT UNFORGETTABLE SPRING, Lord Kaga became a hermit.

Buck-Teeth was amazed at the news. The idea of a *daimyo* turning his back on the luxury and prestige of his birthright seemed, simply, crazy.

"There must be some mistake," Buck-Teeth told the innkeeper. "Surely you don't mean Lord Kaga of Shinano Province!"

The innkeeper, a flabby, black-bearded bear of a fellow, cracked a yellow-toothed smile. "No mistake. It's Kaga. Living on the mountain like a common beggar."

"Which mountain?" Kuro asked.

The innkeeper flung open the wooden shutters of the window next to the table where Buck-Teeth and Kuro sat sipping tea. He pointed at white-capped Mount Fuji.

"*That* mountain," he said.

"But why?" Buck-Teeth wanted to know.

The innkeeper scratched his head. "Obviously, Lord Kaga has gone insane."

"Obviously," Kuro agreed.

When the innkeeper left to prepare their food, Buck-Teeth leaned close to Kuro, nose to nose, and said, "Let's visit him!"

"Who? *Kaga*?" The Poet in Black frowned. "You heard the man. He's out of his mind. Could be dangerous."

Buck-Teeth remembered how Lord Kaga had helped his parents, releasing them from the strangulation of the rice tax. He felt obligated to the old fart.

"Well, *I'm* going," he announced.

Kuro sighed. Regrettably, his young friend had yet to grasp the concept of *mujō*. All is transitory inside Buddha's dream. Nothing abides, certainly not ties to a tyrant like Kaga. But Buck-Teeth's mind was made up, so what was the use of arguing?

"Very well. Tomorrow, we'll climb Mount Fuji," Kuro said.

"Like the snail!" Buck-Teeth added excitedly, recalling Master Cup-of-Tea's famous haiku on the subject.

"Yes, Buck-Teeth. Like the snail."

***

Lord Kaga wasn't hard to find. Buck-Teeth and Kuro simply kept to the main road that zigzagged up the slope of the sacred mountain. Along the way, they asked everyone they met—mostly pilgrims—where the crazy ex-*daimyo* lived. Many seemed to know and eagerly offered, along with directions, gossipy tidbits, like:

"They say he isn't of flesh and blood anymore, but a restless ghost."

"I heard that in meditation his whole body glows, fire blazes 'round his head, and he levitates!"

"I heard him one night when the moon was full, up there, all alone, howling like a wolf...And the wolves answered!"

"He's *baka* all right. A mad fool. *I'll* take his money!"

And so on.

Buck-Teeth's curiosity grew and grew.

"Do you think any of it's true, Kuro, what they say about Lord Kaga?"

"I don't know, Buck-Teeth. Why don't you ask him?" Kuro pointed at a grotto of boulders. Smoke tendrils rose from a small wood fire. Over that fire, a disheveled, burly, naked figure hunched. The former *daimyo* of Shinano Province, the very Kaga.

"Welcome, boys!" he bellowed without looking up from the small fish he was cooking. "Enter!"

Buck-Teeth and Kuro gingerly negotiated the maze of rocks and tree trunks, standing and fallen, until they reached the clearing where the little fire danced. There they knelt, facing Kaga.

"Lord Kaga," Buck-Teeth said. "It's good to see you."

"We'll have none of that 'lord' nonsense," he said as he slowly, carefully rotated his fish on a stick. It looked small enough to be eaten in one bite.

"I've retired from *that* life," he added.

Kuro, usually so aloof to all the empty illusions this illusory universe has to offer, succumbed to curiosity. "What *happened* to you? You had everything. Power. Riches. Glory. Such things pass so quickly in this shitty life; why on earth would you give them up before you had to?'

Kaga's haggard, weather-beaten face turned grim. His eyes looked hard and cold as the rocks that filled his mountain grotto.

"I suppose you've heard of Lady Plum, the famous beauty of Edo?"

"I thought you were over her!" Buck-Teeth exclaimed. He remembered that summer years ago, ninety-nine days of lovelorn haiku, ninety-nine manuscripts consigned by Cup-of-Tea to cow piles. But on the hundredth day, Kaga's breakthrough poem had broken through:

> the old fart
> stacks the winter
> kindling

"Ah, my young friend," Kaga sighed. "I thought so, too. But the Lady Plum had other ideas."

He lapsed into silence. The tiny morsel of fish had burnt to a charcoal nub.

"Once this dinner's cooked," he said, finally, "we'll have a feast, we three, and I'll tell you all about it."

A Sunday in September

A BRIGHT, CLOUD-MOTTLED SKY. A warm breeze stirring soupy air. Leaves of ancient live-oaks shivered. The ghostly drapery of Spanish moss, whispery soft, danced.

September in New Orleans. Ah, and a Sunday!

I, of course, was deep into a haiku walk, haikuing.

On automatic pilot, my tramping feet carried me body and soul into the green, tree-lined City Park, a favorite and fecund poetic location.

> petting
> each other's dog
> strangers

I stopped at the "Peristyle," a white-columned picnic pavilion. Four concrete lions lounged on wide steps that dropped into the still, green pond. For fun, I clambered onto one of the sun-warmed lions and straddled it, cowboy-style.

"Gidyap!" I joked.

My antics frightened a turtle, sending him—plop!— down to the murky depths, a haiku inspiration for sure. I whipped out my hip-pocket pad.

> down periscope
> dive! dive!
> turtle

It was a scene for a postcard, and I was in it, riding a lion—but something was missing; this I felt deep in my heart-mind, my *kokoro*. I felt—empty. But why? I had a great job with summers off and plenty of flexible time for poetic ramblings such as today's. I was healthy, happy, and cranking out haiku.

"What *is* it, then?" I asked out loud. The lions weren't talking. Geese and mallards, cruising on the water, revealed nothing. An idle quack. A honk.

I slid off the king of beasts and continued my trek.

"pardon our dust"
the fire ants build
their city

I strolled with a puzzled heart. Could it be my womanlessness, I wondered, that caused this sudden, aching sense of *absence*? My sojourn in a romantic wasteland was going on two years now, although, upon my return from Japan, I had made a half-ass effort to keep in touch with Yumi. Yet, after a few vapid phone calls and letters, I discovered—and I think she did too—we had precious little in common.

A crow attempted to land on a dead branch just a few feet from me. The branch snapped and fell. Wildly flapping, ebony wings caught air, and he flew off. Was he embarrassed?

too fat for that branch
crack!
crow

My feet carried me out of the park, down oak-shaded Carrollton Avenue to Parkside Tavern. Several outdoor tables under a green canvas awning beckoned me.

To sit, definitely.

And to drink, perhaps.

Which, very soon, I was doing. Guzzling one beer. Guzzling two.

> getting drunk
> on my arm
> the tavern mosquitoes

I felt warm inside, benevolent even, allowing the mosquitoes to nip my arms without smacking them dead, as I normally would have done. I imagined that my alcohol-laced blood was getting *them* high, that my arms served as their tavern, just as I sat guzzling in mine.

Tavern in a tavern, I thought to myself and chuckled.

A low-riding, red car screeched to a stop in front of my table. Its black-tinted passenger window rolled down. A pretty face with a pointy chin appeared in that window. It was the face of the driver, bending across the front seat to peer at me, and to smile.

It was the face of my ex-fiancée, Natasha!

The something missing.

"Whatcha doin'?" she chirped.

Lady Plum's Floating World

THEY ATE THEIR "MEAL" of the tiny, burnt-to-charcoal fish. A nibble for Buck-Teeth, a nibble for Kuro, and a half-nibble for the naked hermit, the once mighty, once lord, Kaga.

"Ah," he said, smacking his lips with pleasure. "That hit the spot!"

"We appreciate your kind generosity, Lord Kaga." Buck-Teeth bowed.

"I told you, Buck-Teeth, I'm not 'lord' anymore." Kaga shook a bony finger at the young poet. "If you wish to add an honorific to my name, let it be 'fool'. I insist!"

"Fool Kaga," Kuro muttered under his breath and smiled at the funny sound it made in Japanese: *baka-na-kaga*.

"Now," Kaga the Fool said. "I will tell you boys a story. A story of a man, a woman, and a tattoo. Care to hear it?"

"Oh, yes!" Buck-Teeth said.

"It began, this story did, in Yoshiwara."

Kuro nodded knowingly, but Buck-Teeth looked puzzled. Kuro observed, "Our young friend here is not familiar with the 'floating world' of Yoshiwara."

"Then I shall describe it for you," Kaga said. "Yoshiwara, Buck-Teeth, is the Shogun's licensed brothel district—a world unto itself, surrounded by high walls and crowned with sharp stakes. In it, three thousand of our land's most ravishing beauties ply their trades. Dancers, singers, *samisen* players, courtesans, *geisha*, tea-girls. A floating world, indeed. Ah, Buck-Teeth, you should visit some day. A young man like you would appreciate such a place. But back to my story.

"Several years ago I met my Lady Plum there, in

Yoshiwara. But she was no common, shall we say, 'woman of the evening'. Oh, no. She was, like her mother before her, the most exquisite, expensive bit of bewitching female company that you could ever, in your wildest imaginings, imagine. Courtesans of *her* rank expect to be wooed with love letters and gifts: jewels, works of art, nightingales in golden cages. And, for the most demanding of them, as Lady Plum surely was, poetry. At first our courtship went well. I lavished presents on her. Many an evening we sat on the moon-soaked verandah of her mansion, sipping sake, surrounded by serving girls who entertained us with dance and music. Then one night she demanded something that I could not give. In a cold voice and with colder eyes, she insisted that I compose a haiku in her honor. Until and unless I did so, she said, she could never offer her whole self to me.

"This is why I traveled to Kashiwabara the summer I met you, Buck-Teeth, to learn poetic art from the master, from Cup-of-Tea."

Kaga fell silent. The little wood fire had dwindled to a few glowing embers. The icy feel of the approaching darkness made Buck-Teeth gather his travel coat tightly around his shoulders and neck. He wondered how Kaga, nude, endured the biting wind that swirled over the mountain.

Kuro encouraged Kaga to continue. "So to capture your lady's heart, you studied haiku?"

Kaga nodded. His eyes smoldered red. His great jaw clenched. For a second, he looked like the old Kaga. Terrible. Cruel. As if he could crush whole villages in his iron fist.

"The tattoo," he said, forcing out the words with a hiss between his teeth. "Let me tell you about *that*."

The Tattoo

I got up from my table and strolled over to the cherry-red car.

"What are *you* doing in New Orleans?"

"I live here now," my former True Love replied. "In fact, in this neighborhood. I've been here six months."

Her words cut like a knife to the heart.

Six months, I thought. *And you never called?*

But before I could order up the appropriate emotion from my emotional memory bank—I was torn between "seething rage" and "righteous self-pity"—she asked, "Can I join you? Catch up on old times?"

My insides melted to buttery mush. I could never refuse this woman. *My* woman, once.

"Why not?"

Natasha joined me at my little table under the green awning. We idled away the afternoon. We talked. We flirted. We drank beer.

And we even, softly, kissed.

***

After his matriculation from Cup-of-Tea's haiku school in the meadow behind Trash House, Lord Kaga had celebrated with a wonderful fireworks display at the lake. But you knew that.

His realization that he was just a silly old fart had steeled the daimyo in his resolve to forget about Lady Plum. That spring, when he returned to his mansion in Edo, the Shogun's bustling capital, Lord Kaga achieved his objective. He managed to purge from heart and mind the woman he had fixated on for so long.

And so he lived happily, until...

A sleek, red palanquin lurched to a stop in front of the teahouse where Lord Kaga sat sipping with friends and concubines. The palanquin, balanced on the sturdy shoulders of four sun-darkened runners, hovered in the air, casting a deep shadow over the *daimyo's* table. After a long, dramatic pause, a little black window shutter slid open, and a slender, ivory-white arm fell out. To Kaga's amazement, on that arm, in thick, blue characters, he read his own name.

He recognized both the palanquin and the arm. They belonged to Lady Plum. On her soft, sweet, precious skin, "Kaga" shouted in bold calligraphy for all the world to see!

He was ecstatic. The arm withdrew, the window slid shut, and the palanquin drifted away, but the meaning of the tattoo display was not lost on Lord Kaga. Lady Plum wanted him back! She *must* want him back, if she had gone so far as to have his name inked into her flesh!

He could hardly contain his joy. His companions, at least the discerning ones in the party, understood exactly what had just transpired but politely deferred from commenting on it. Lord Kaga bellowed for sake, then commanded that everyone in the teahouse, everyone on the street, including all passersby, enjoy a cup at his expense. And then he did the unthinkable: on the spot, he granted his youngest concubine her freedom.

"Return to your village, little one. Your parents' debt is settled!"

New Blood

THOUGH I HAD FEARED that our little writing group had outlived its purpose, our once-a-week, Thursday afternoon club clung to existence much like Cup-of-Tea's dog, Scruffy, might to a bone. Melanie quit (as abruptly as she had vanished from Old Japan), but we soon replaced her with new blood: quiet, introspective Paul, the same Paul who participated in the sushi restaurant *renga* party described in an earlier chapter.

Our new writing cadre line-up lacked its former gender balance, but thrived with Paul's presence, as if reborn. This might be due to the fact that our newest member *was* new. New eyes scanned our precious drafts. A new voice softly, almost apologetically, offered gentle suggestions as to how we might fiddle with this or that word or sentence, such as *this* sentence, which, in fact, has been greatly fiddled with, thanks to Paul.

I explained to him at the very first meeting he attended that this text of mine is no mere invention on my part, that, in fact, I am transcribing in it the gushing ramblings of some invisible Buddha from Beyond.

"I see," Paul said, stroking his sandy-red beard, not a trace of disbelief or irony in his tone.

Last Thursday, I shared with our reborn group my description of Lord Kaga glimpsing his old flame's arm with his name on it, tattooed in blue.

"...Return to your village, little one. Your parents' debt is settled!" I finished reading and laid the chapter on Micky's cluttered coffee table.

Chaz was first to respond.

"That's it?"

"What do you mean?" I asked.

He rubbed his whisker-stubbled chin. "I mean, it's an important scene. Lady Plum, after months of teasing us, finally makes her appearance, and all we get to see is her *arm*?"

"It was rather a letdown," Micky agreed. Her cool, gray eyes peered at me over her reading glasses.

Paul, usually careful to lace his comments with all kinds of softeners, such as "it seems to me" or "another way of looking at it" or "perhaps you might try," bluntly joined the bandwagon.

"It's slight," he said.

"*Slight?*"

He cleared his throat. "I expected Lady Plum to do more," he explained. "Step down from that palanquin, perhaps. Say something."

"Or perhaps send Lord Kaga a note," Micky suggested. "You've silenced the female voice in your text. Up to this point, Lady Plum has been somewhat of an *aporia*."

"A what?" I asked.

"An *aporia*, an absence. A something missing."

Chaz nodded. "I don't know a fancy name for it, but I feel cheated as a reader. You've built up my expectations; I want to *see* this woman!"

I didn't know what to say, so I rattled off my standard disclaimer. "You all know I'm just the Buddha's stenographer in this thing."

"Buddha's not a member of this group," Micky observed dryly.

"Well, how would *you* write it?" I snapped.

Just then, a wonderful idea occurred to me.

"That's it!" I exclaimed. "Each of you will write the scene at the teahouse the way *you* think it happened!"

They stared at me blankly.

"That'll be my next chapter, like when a jazz musician steps offstage to allow his guest performers to jam. The next chapter, *you'll* write. I'll step down and let you, my guests, improvise!"

They looked at me as if I were crazy. But a week later, when we reconvened, I received three new, neatly word-processed versions of what "really" happened that spring afternoon, long ago in Old Japan.

My Guest Writers Sit In

CHAZ'S RENDITION OF THE TEAHOUSE scene was fraught with the same violent imagery that bloodies the pages of his own text-in-progress, his science-fiction thriller about mutated Arkansan monsters.

***

Kaga glanced up from his tea just in time. The ceiling of the teahouse imploded; splinters of wood and shards of blue enamel sleeted down with a dozen massive human shapes.

Helmeted, armed samurai, swords drawn, surrounded him.

My enemies! he thought, then smiled grimly.

"It's a good day to die!" he roared, springing to battle stance, while in one fluid motion sliding both *katana* and *wakizashi* out of their long and short scabbards.

The copper tang of adrenaline filled his mouth. He spat, then charged.

Parry, thrust, jab. Metal blurs sliced the air. An enemy eyeball popped free. An enemy throat flapped open like a red book. An enemy hand still gripping its sword spun 'round and 'round in a bloody mist.

The battle tumbled out of the teahouse, over crashing tables and shattering china, onto the street crowded with passersby. People screamed, running desperately to avoid the swords ripping the air.

A pause. Dust settled. Eight of Kaga's attackers lay dead or dying. Four survivors, shoulder to shoulder, pressed forward *en masse*.

He taunted them, "Come on!"

In that instant, the assassins lost their collective nerve, turned, and ran, colliding with an approaching palanquin.

The car tilted and toppled. A bundle of red silk spilled out its door into the air, into Lord Kaga's waiting arms.

"Nice of you to drop by, Lady Plum," he said.

***

Micky's version, like her own autobiographical novel, was filled with clipped sentence fragments, dripping with angst.

***

In her stately palanquin. Floating through crowded, narrow streets. The Shogun's history-drenched capital.

"There's nothing, Takako, nothing!" Lady Plum shivered.

Her serving girl nodded mutely. Hunched across from her in the darkness.

"A pointless abyss . . . Death . . . Meaningless suffering!"

Takako, her face pale as the plague victims of Camus, still said nothing.

"See this?" Lady Plum held out her arm. Revealed the tattoo. Still raw. Each pore resentful of the needle that had pierced it with pigment.

"*His* name, Takako, not mine! Inscribed on the page of myself . . ."

Takako, so pale. Frozen in darkness.

"I didn't ask for too much, did I? Are the heroes dead? Look at me, Takako. I've become *his* text, *his* discourse! All I wanted was a lousy haiku!"

The palanquin lurched to a stop.

"We're there." Lady Plum sighed. She slid the window open a crack and peered out.

"There he is. Fat and satisfied. Sitting with his cronies and whores. Not a thought of me in his vacant head!"

She opened the shutter all the way. Thrust out her arm. Dangled it far enough to display an absurd emblem that all, especially he, would misconstrue.

"That'll do it," she told Takako, then shouted to her carriers, "Go!"

***

Paul's version of the scene, though unfinished, exhibits the same warm, rambling style as the memoir he's currently writing, about growing up in Mississippi.

***

My best buddy in those days was the fish merchant's chubby, gregarious son. We called him

Maguro, "Tuna," not only because he packed generous slabs of smoked tuna for all our outings, but because, perhaps due to his daily diet, the boy *smelled* like tuna, actually reeked of it.

I looked up to Maguro as a leader and mentor, though we were the same age. In those days, size counted for plenty, so it just seemed natural that the largest boy on our block should lead the gang.

One particular spring afternoon, Maguro decided to play a prank on some of the palanquin bearers who marched up and down the narrow street, hauling loads of the rich and famous.

"We'll trick 'em, pal," he said, his smile missing a front tooth.

How he lost that tooth deserves telling.

Maguro's father, the fishmonger, was a strict and religious man . . .

The Sex Chapter

FEELING HAPPY AND DRUNK and thrilled by the warm, wet kiss we had shared under the green canvas awning, I suggested to Natasha, "Let's go to my place."

Before I could finish the sentence, she was standing. "I'll drive," she said.

I understood that gleam in my ex-one-and-only's eyes. She wanted me. And I, *baka* ("fool") that I was, am, planned to oblige.

But first there was the matter of the ring.

Back when we were happily, I thought, engaged, I had incurred some serious debt to purchase for my bride-to-be a full-carat solitaire diamond ring with a wide, white gold band. Unfortunately, before I finished paying for this token of undying love, love died. And Natasha claimed, during our last, weird, long-distance phone conversation, that she had "lost" the ring.

Now we were naked, rolling in my futon, remembering each other's bodies with hungry fingers and tongues. I *had* to ask; I was burning to know.

"Tash," I whispered in her ear, "what *really* happened? To the ring?"

She clamped her arms around me, pressed her sharp chin hard into the crook of my neck. Her body trembled, then violently shook.

She was crying.

***

Lord Kaga planned to pay a visit to the incomparable Lady Plum of Yoshiwara, who had displayed on her lovely arm the *daimyo's* very name.

He didn't go right away. That would have made him seem too eager.

I'll wait a week, he thought, *then just happen to visit Yoshiwara, and while there, just happen to stop at Lady Plum's.*

It was an excellent plan of amorous attack, or so he believed.

He reached the outskirts of Yoshiwara on his

private barge. As his rowers heaved their oars, Lord Kaga's heart thumped with anticipation.

The rowers docked the boat, and the daimyo hurried to complete the last leg of the journey, riding a fine, rented horse across a causeway through the flooded rice fields. He soon caught sight of the tall, spiked wall of the pleasure district.

The gatekeeper, recognizing him, smiled. The gate swung open.

Lord Kaga entered.

***

I had received no coherent answer to the ring question, just sobs and broken phrases like "so stupid," "can't explain," "I messed up," and so on. No matter. Making love with my love after all this time was something I couldn't stand to delay for a second longer.

A perfect, snug fit. Warm and wonderful. I had forgotten how warm, how wonderful.

Now I broke down—cried and shook as fiercely as she had just done.

Like an old fart.

A fool.

A Kaga.

***

When he returned to his barge, Lord Kaga at first said nothing to his crew. His face grim and drained of blood, shoulders strangely stooped, he boarded the boat and collapsed onto pillows.

After several minutes of staring into space, he roared to his rowers, "Home!"

He wanted to forget the brittle sound of Lady Plum's laughter and the sight of her in her blood-red kimono on the verandah, where she had been playing a game of poem cards with a doting customer.

It wasn't the fact that she was entertaining that had destroyed him. After all, Lord Kaga had made no appointment with her tonight, had silently crept to her verandah, bathed in the blue light of dangling globe lanterns.

She hadn't noticed him, so engrossed was she in the game, giggling and joking with her guest whom Kaga recognized to be one of Edo's wealthiest merchants.

It wasn't jealousy. Jealousy, he could have handled.

What the daimyo could not handle was her *arm*. That same white arm that she had thrust out a palanquin window just seven days ago. A white arm that now was nothing *but* white.

No name on it. No tattoo.

The tattoo he had glimpsed last week hadn't been a real one, he now realized, but rather the cruel joke of one of the cruelest hearts in the Shogun's cruel, cruel city.

Next day, he left Edo and became a hermit.

Mrs. Moray

I realize, to my chagrin, that I have been so involved relating the ins and outs of mine and Lord Kaga's romantic dalliances, I've neglected to offer much advice, lately, on how to write haiku. So I suppose that now is good a time as any to discuss the matter of structure.

But first, an anecdote.

My seventh grade English teacher, Mrs. Moray, loved to enlighten us with all sorts of creative projects. Once, in October, she had us write poems about falling leaves. Suzy Weisdecker, the smart, mousy girl in the front row who wore thick, horn-rimmed glasses and for whom I had a pathetic crush, outdid the rest of the class, as usual. Her poem, a page of perfectly rhyming couplets—"brown" with "down," "fall" with "all," "trees" with "breeze," and so on—was framed by gold and red maple leaves that Suzy had ingeniously stapled to the page.

My own poem that day was a macabre ballad about a man being chased through misty woods by a zombie. In the dramatic final verse, the zombie caught the man and devoured his brain. Chaz would have loved it.

After Mrs. Moray finished praising Suzy's leaf-framed masterpiece, I was certain that she would mention *my* poem next. In those days I already considered myself a writer. But Mrs. Moray didn't laud my bloody ballad. She just handed it back to me with a "D-" scrawled on the page (and my poet's soul) in red-as-her-lipstick magic marker. As I took the paper from her fingers that held it at arm's length, as if it were a dead rat, she said, "I see *you* have a warped little mind!"

Mrs. Moray's next poetic project that year was haiku. She told us to go out "into Nature" one weekend and write "haiku poems."

"Make sure that your poem is three lines long. The first line must contain five syllables. The second line, seven syllables. And the third line, class, needs five syllables, like the first. Five, seven, five." She wrote these important numbers on the chalkboard. "Any questions?"

I had a whole lot of questions but knew better than to ask them. With all that syllable-counting and Nature-mentioning, who could possibly squeeze in subject matter that, in those days, I considered "cool," such as monsters, dinosaurs, or spies?

Not surprisingly, it was Suzy, poetess with a staple gun, who wrote the best haiku of the class. Indeed, to hear Mrs. Moray talk about it, it was the best haiku ever written, at home or abroad. Its topic was her mother's rose bush. Around the margins, Suzy had stapled a heart of crimson petals.

Years later, when I began seriously to study the instant art of haiku, I came to realize that Mrs. Moray had put the cart way before the horse when she taught that the main thing about haiku is counting syllables. There are two problems with this approach. The first is the fact that haiku *spirit* is the essence of the thing, not this or that number of sounds.

The second problem has to do with language. Japanese words tend to have more syllables than English ones. Take for example, this Cup-of-Tea poem:

147

> uma no he ni
> fuki tobasaruru
> hotaru kana

The literal translation of the three phrases follows: (1) by horse's fart (2) blown (3) firefly! Notice that the middle phrase, so very long in Japanese, requires only one syllable of English to say the same thing; *fuki tobasaruru* becomes, simply, "blown."

Suppose now, that we take Mrs. Moray's advice and attempt to translate this haiku using seventeen syllables:

> by the horse's fart
> blown far away, far away . . .
> the little firefly

Too much fluff, don't you think? A better rule than syllable counting would be to insist only that the poem be readable in an easy breath. Take an ordinary breath and say your haiku. If you're not gasping for air at the end, it's probably OK.

Here's my best shot at translating the above Cup-of-Tea poem:

> blown away
> by the horse's fart
> firefly

In addition to the one breath rule, I would argue for only one other structural requirement for a haiku

to be a haiku: it must end in a revelation, a punch line,
an image/thought that makes you say, "Ahhh!"

faces in the next car
one
a Chihuahua
—me

it's a cold world—
goose egg
in the lake
—Kuro

outside the tavern
two dogs
wait
—Mido

a red glint
in its bubble-eye
fly
—Buck-Teeth

lightning flash—
only the dog's face
is innocent
—Cup-of-Tea

149

Last Chapter

AFTER OUR TEAR-DRENCHED LOVEMAKING, I waited a week before calling Natasha. I didn't want to phone her right away, didn't want to seem desperate; wanted, this time around, to do everything right.

What prevented our getting back together? I loved her, and I believed that she loved me. How else to account for the weeping-fest we had shared in my futon? I figured, if it wasn't love, we would have just "cleaned out our pipes," that is, enjoyed the sex, as Cup-of-Tea once urged the flies in his hut to do:

while I'm gone
enjoy your screwing
flies

Geography, now, was no problem. Natasha resided in the Crescent City, in my own neighborhood, in fact. Those years she had lived in Nashville, where she had attended medical school, had seen the collapse and fizzle of our relationship. I naturally blamed our break-up on the distance between us. But now, the way she had pressed her body to mine, burrowing her pointy chin into the crook of my neck, she wanted me back— I was sure of it!

Pondering it all week, I even came up with a positive spin on the fact that my soul mate had been living in New Orleans for six months without calling or attempting to see me. The reason? She feared rejection! But Great Buddha had intervened and had sent her cherry-red sports car rocketing up Carrollton Avenue at the precise moment that I sat under a green awning gulping beer and letting the mosquitoes prick.

***

The phone rang once. The phone rang twice. I felt fluttery inside, ready and eager to begin the rest of my life.

A man answered.

"Who is it?" His voice was gravelly, filled with macho gruffness.

"A friend of Natasha's. Is she there?"

"Hold on," he growled.

Her voice was light and perky. "That's my new friend who answered," she gushed. "He's really nice. We met through the personals."

And on she chatted about his wonderfulness. How she felt at ease with him. As if she had known him all her life. How they planned to move to Massachusetts together, in December.

"I'm so happy," she bubbled.

"I'm happy *for you*," I lied.

And that was that.

***

But I thank Natasha. She inspired this book, after all, since I began writing it as therapy for my crushed heart.

And I thank the Buddha for dreaming me, and for

dreaming up the day that I happened upon the Puffin paperback edition of *Buck-Teeth's Diary,* introducing me to haiku and changing everything. Thank you, Buddha, for dreaming me, everything, and everyone! Amen.

Kuro was right. All this passes, and sooner than we think.

And wild, green Mido was right, too: the moment is worth dancing in.

Shiro was right to keep his mouth shut.

And as for Cup-of-Tea, now happily married to the lovely, heavy-lidded Kiku, I wish him well. His words and his silences have always been equally eloquent.

Enough. There's a world floating outside these cracked apartment walls. A bright September day just made for haiku.

I think I'll go out and scribble.

Afterword

Many thanks to the two Jims: Jim Cypher for proofreading and believing, and Jim Kacian for editing and design—*arigato gozaimashita!*

The only real poet quoted in this book has been Cup-of-Tea (Kobayashi Issa), whose haiku I have taken from *Issa zenshu* (Nagano: Shinano Mainichi Shimbunsha, 1979). Some of my translations of these haiku first appeared in my book, *Issa: Cup-of-Tea Poems; Selected Haiku of Kobayashi Issa* (Berkeley: Asian Humanities Press, 1991). Some of the original haiku in the present book were first published in *Modern Haiku* and in *Frogpond* magazine. Excerpted chapters of *Haiku Guy* have appeared in *Modern Haiku, Frogpond,* and *Xavier Review.*